THE GOLDEN AGE
YORKSHIRE STEAM
AND BEYOND

MEMORIES OF THE 50s, 60s & 70s

BARNSLEY • LEEDS • DONCASTER • YORK • DARLINGTON • PENISTONE

K3 2-6-0 61808 passes through Hazelhead station near Penistone with an excursion in 1953.

A goods train approaches the West Silkstone junction from Barnsley, pre 1952.

THE GOLDEN AGE OF YORKSHIRE STEAM
AND BEYOND
MEMORIES OF THE 50s, 60s & 70s

BARNSLEY • LEEDS • DONCASTER • YORK • DARLINGTON • PENISTONE

Edited by Peter Hadfield

PEN & SWORD
TRANSPORT

AN IMPRINT OF PEN & SWORD BOOKS LTD.
YORKSHIRE – PHILADELPHIA

Barnsley – Wakefield service at Low Barugh, hauled by 4MT 2-6-0 43137, 20 July 1966.

First published in Great Britain in 2020 by
Pen & Sword Transport
An imprint of Pen & Sword Books Ltd
47 Church Street
Barnsley
South Yorkshire
S70 2AS

Copyright © Peter Hadfield, 2020

ISBN 9781526765888

The right of Peter Hadfield to be identified as the author of this work has been asserted by him in accordance with the Copyright, Designs and Patents Act 1988. All rights reserved. No part of this publication may be reproduced or transmitted in any form or by any means, electronic or mechanical, including photocopy, recording or any information storage and retrieval system, without the prior written permission of the publisher, nor by way of trade or otherwise shall it be lent, re-sold, hired out or otherwise circulated without the publisher's prior consent in any form of binding or cover other than that in which it is published and without a similar condition including this condition being imposed on the subsequent purchaser.

Typeset by Pen & Sword Books Ltd
Printed and bound by Replika Press Pvt. Ltd.

Pen & Sword Books Ltd incorporates the imprints of Pen & Sword Archaeology, Atlas, Aviation, Battleground, Discovery, Family History, History, Maritime, Military, Naval, Politics, Railways, Select, Social History, Transport, True Crime, and Claymore Press, Frontline Books, Leo Cooper, Praetorian Press, Remember When, Seaforth Publishing and Wharncliffe.

For a complete list of Pen and Sword titles please contact
Pen and Sword Books Limited
47 Church Street, Barnsley, South Yorkshire, S70 2AS, England
E-mail: enquiries@pen-and-sword.co.uk
Website: www.pen-and-sword.co.uk

CONTENTS

Introduction
6

Royston Shed – 1962-1967
Gerald Darby
9

Cudworth Station & Beyond – 1950s
Ken Gambles
28

York Station and visits to Darlington and Doncaster – 1950s and early 1960s
Malcolm Parker
60

A Train-spotter's Paradise – 1950s-1960s
Jeff Hodgson
98

Stairfoot, Barnsley to Doncaster, The Centres, The Specials & Barry
Peter Hadfield
110

Penistone 1950s
Aldred Bostwick
136

Barnsley & Beyond – 1950s
Michael Watkin
144

The Smoke, The Smell, The Steam – 1948-1955
Brian Mathers
153

The journeys from Barnsley in the 1950s
158

INTRODUCTION

RECALLING AMONG FRIENDS the trainspotting memories of our youth, I was gently reminded that we were members of the last generation to be able to recall the days when steam was still king. It was a time of youth and innocence, not realising then how the railway scene would change so rapidly. Our beloved steam locomotives would be gone, consigned to the scrapheap, along with an extreme rationalisation of our railway system with the closure of many lines and stations. We were lucky to live through a golden age of our railways, when steam was still king and the services and stations provided us with an excellent choice of destinations within the UK.

With that in mind, and being aware of those no longer with us who had not written down their experiences, I decided to gather a collection of railway memories of friends, colleagues, and indeed my own, for future generations to savour. I am indebted to the following people whose contributions in this book will hopefully stir the memories of those interested in railways.

Gerald Darby
Gerald was a fireman at Royston shed from the early 1960s to the closure of the shed to steam on 4 November 1967. He left the railway for a period of time before rejoining in the capacity of a signalman, working in that role until retirement.

Ken Gambles
At the age of five Ken moved from Grimethorpe to live on Barnsley Road, Cudworth, later to become Pontefract Road, Lundwood, and here it was that for the next decade or so he delighted in the railways nearby: the Midland line at Cudworth with its branch to Barnsley, and the ex- Hull & Barnsley on the last stage of its journey to Stairfoot from Hull. Along with football, trainspotting was a source of tremendous enjoyment for him and was also vital in the process of growing up, being educational and helping to forge independence through travel to Doncaster, Leeds and York for example. How wonderful it would be to go back in time to spend one hour watching steam again in its heyday.

Introduction   7

Malcolm Parker

Malcolm was born in York in 1948. He lived north of the city in the village of Haxby, where he went to junior school before transferring to Archbishop Holgate Grammar School in 1959. After studying at the University of Hull, he followed a career in local government, moving to South Yorkshire in 1974. When he took early retirement in 2002 he became joint owner of a wildlife tour company, organising trips to all parts of the world and leading safaris to several East African countries including Kenya and Tanzania. Now fully retired, and living in Penistone, he still enjoys travelling and is involved in a number of volunteer activities, one of which is at the National Rail Museum in his former home city.

Jeff Hodgson

Jeff lived in Cudworth, with a magnificent view of the station. His memories of Cudworth, Leeds, Doncaster and York are unique. On leaving school he spent his working life in the glass industry until retirement. He still enjoys the railway scene, visiting the centres, travelling on the steam specials and viewing them whenever possible.

Peter Hadfield

Peter spent his formative and early adult years living in Kendray, near Barnsley, and attended the local schools which were, and in the case of his old junior school still is, close to the Barnsley–Sheffield, and former Chapeltown loop lines, along with the former Barnsley–Doncaster line at Stairfoot. From an early age he was enthralled by the local railway scene before moving onto the more glamorous railway centres. The railway scene today, although not as it was, still invokes a passion after all these years.

Aldred Bostwick

Aldred was born in Hoylandswaine, near Penistone, and has resided there all his life. He has worked in the insurance industry all his working life. His passion for railways is centred on the Penistone area, both in steam and electric traction days.

Michael Watkin
Michael spent his early life in Kendray, near Barnsley, and was a keen railway enthusiast from an early age, trainspotting in and around the local area before venturing to Sheffield, Wath, Leeds and Doncaster. Michael and his family emigrated to Australia in 1961. Apart from the Australian railways, he has always maintained a keen interest in the UK railways, and his memories are based on his early life in the UK.

Brian Mathers
Brian was born and raised in the neighbourhood of Cundy Cross, near Barnsley. He attended the local junior school and Barnsley Central School. His passion for railways was invoked at nearby Stairfoot and Cudworth before progressing further afield. On leaving school his working life was spent in the carpentry trade initially, followed by the mining industry, and finally twenty-six years for the post office. He represented his community as a local councillor for a number of years, later becoming Mayor of Barnsley. He is chairman of a local heritage group and a member of local choirs.

Acknowledgements
I am indebted to the following people who have given permission to use photographs and extracts from book publications: Les Nixon, Peter Buck, Chris Sharp, Peter Hogarth, Ian Allan Publishing Ltd, British Railways Motive Power Depots, LMS, Eastern and North-Eastern Regions, Steam World, P.J. Lynch, A. Ripley, Peter Waller and Rail Photoprints, Dawn Cover Productions, R.K. Blencowe, A. Godfrey and A.L. Brown.

While every effort has been made to trace the copyright holders of featured photographs, this has not always proved possible because of the antiquity of the images.

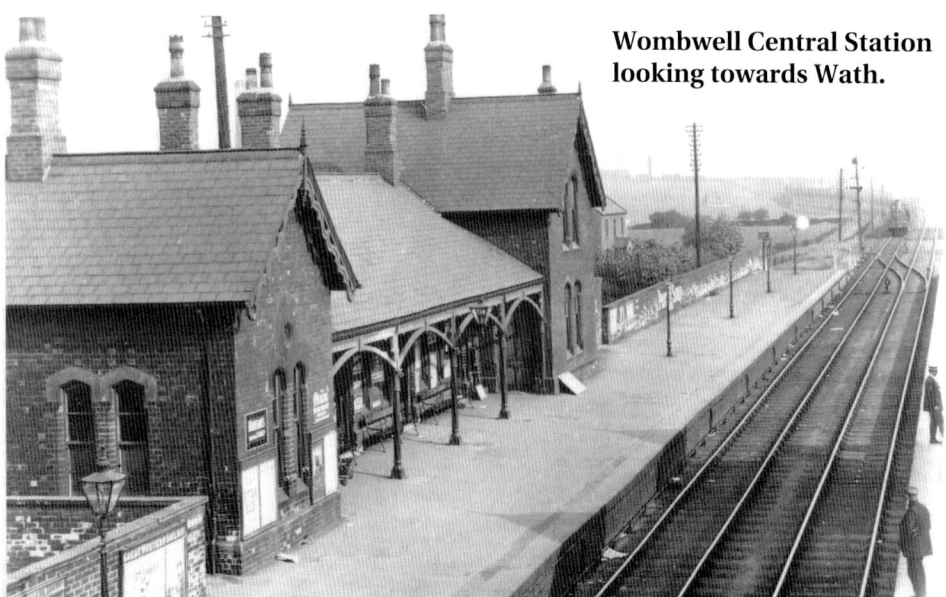

Wombwell Central Station looking towards Wath.

ROYSTON SHED
1962–1967

by Gerald Darby

ROYSTON SHED HAD been built by the LMS in 1932 to serve in the main, the local collieries, therefore the main allocation of the engines consisted of freight engines e.g. Stanier 8Fs, Fowler 4Fs and WD Austerities along with a small number of Ivatt tanks, Black Fives, BR Standards, 4-6-0s and 9Fs. The shed was set inside a triangle, used to turn engines as the turntable was situated at Carlton North sidings.

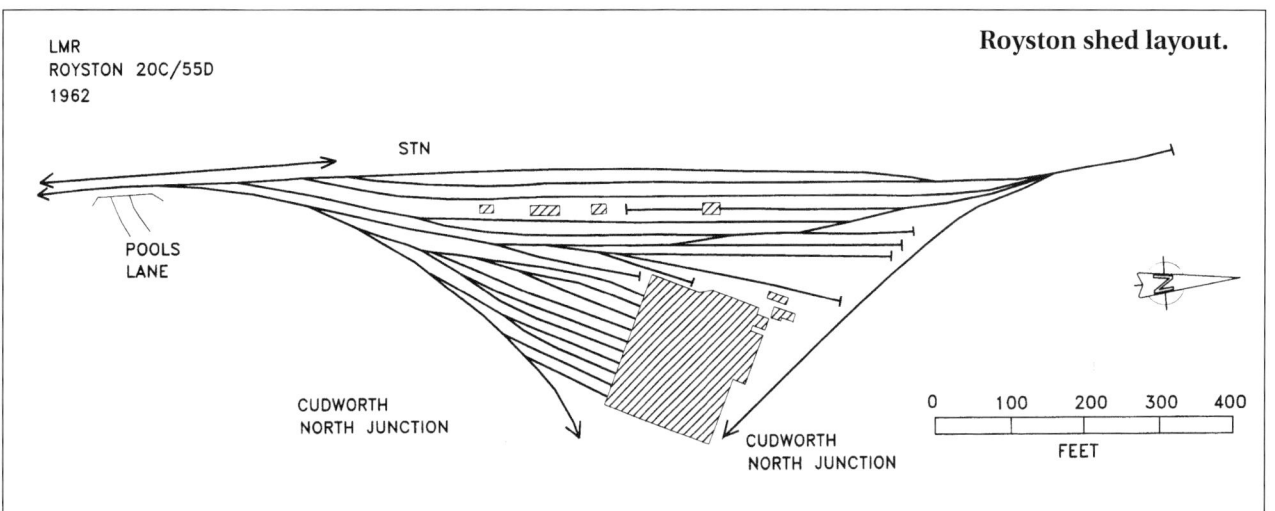

Royston shed layout.

Royston shed as it looked in 1953.

A row of Stanier 8F 2-8-0s', May 1967.
G. Darby

Stanier 8F loco 48076 awaiting its next turn of duty, May 1967. G. Darby

Two 4Fs and a Black 5 on shed, May 1967.
G. Darby

I started work at the shed along with five other lads on 24 April 1962, all of us starting in the role of engine cleaners. I found it a strange feeling walking down the shed yard as there was no fear of being chased out of the shed, for all previous visits had been unofficial. Along with the other lads, we were told to report to the charge hand cleaner Charlie Ellis, then proceeded to the stores van to collect two sets of overall uniforms and jackets, my first grease top hat and the tangerine British Railways badge.

Royston was a ten-road shed and in 1962 things had changed: eight of the roads were dedicated to steam, i.e. one to eight, and roads nine and ten were occupied by 350 horse-powered diesel shunters, which had replaced the Jinties. The shed had the benefit of a mechanical coaler, hopper and ash disposal plant. Shed roads 1 to 8 were capable of holding two 8F locos inside the shed and one or two outside.

3F 0-6-0 43789 in store, 11 October 1959.
R.K. Blencowe

Stanier 8F 2-8-0 48454 on shed with snow plough fitted, May 1967. G. Darby

My first twelve months of working at the shed included engine cleaning and shed labouring duties which consisted of ash pit cleaning and barman's work (replacing the fire bars after fire cleaning). Being a barman or general labouring meant an increase in money. The barman on the early turn would check the engine board to see which engines were stopped for washout, then he would climb into the firebox, clean the clinker off the stay nuts,

Stanier 8F 2-8-0 with its number indiscernible on shed, 1967. G. Darby

Locomotives on the store line, May 1967.

clear ash off the brick arch and replace burnt firebars. When this was done, engines having their fires cleaned would have five or as many firebars as required to be removed to allow ash to be raked into the ashpan, and it was then the barman's job to replace them using a hooked bar then riding on

Gerald Darby on the footplate of 8F 48076.

A classic photograph taken in September/October 1967 of Battle of Britain locomotive 34051 *Winston Churchill* at Royston shed while on its way to Hellifield for storage prior to preservation. The lead engine is BR Standard 73112 *Morgan le Fay* (minus smokebox door) and is being used as a buffer engine. It should have been removed at Rotherham, but clearly wasn't. (G. Darby)

A clean-looking WD Austerity 2-8-0 90650 at Brierley Junction in the late 1950s/ early 1960s.

the engine into the shed. I was barman one day and got to drive my first loco, 4F 43942, into the shed.

The barman's work allowed me plenty of time to help the firemen with fire cleaning and gain knowledge of the shed layout, changing points and engine stabling, all good training for later. At the end of the first twelve months, I spent two weeks with the loco inspector, who tested me on the rules and regulations, working of the locos and the correct way to fire a loco. I passed all the tests and became an engine cleaner, passed to act as a fireman when required. I had passed the tests on a Friday and my first firing job came up on the following Monday.

The lines we worked were the Calder Valley line, the former Hull and Barnsley terminating at Wrangbrook but servicing collieries at Monckton, Upton and Brodsworth, along with sidings at Brierley which gave access to the former Dearne Valley Railway, and Hemsworth for access to the West Riding, Doncaster–Wakefield line. Trains for Brodsworth had to run round at Wrangbrook, shunt into the single line with a token for the line to

Pickburn, where you ran around again for the colliery after handing over the single token to the signalman. We also undertook trip workings from Carlton, servicing Monckton Coke works, Redfearns Glass Works, Monk Bretton Colliery, Manvers Colliery, Houghton Main Colliery, and Wath Yard.

Trains loading from Cudworth Yard North to Wath and beyond, when ready to depart after the siding signal cleared, had a clear road to Stairfoot. The line had a falling gradient to Weetshaw Lane Bridge, then began to climb for a few hundred yards, over the Midland Main Line at Cudworth North Junction, it was then a falling gradient, passing under the line which was the former route of the Cudworth–Barnsley–Cudworth pull-and-push service. This line today, as it did then, still serves the former Redfearns Glass Factory (now Ardagh), but is terminated beyond the factory.

The line passed under Burton Road bridge, running adjacent to the former Monk Bretton Colliery spoil heap, under the A628 Pontefract Road bridge maintaining a falling gradient as it skirted the boundary of Lundwood and onwards to Stairfoot. The line from Cudworth Yard North to Stairfoot Junction station box was the terminus of the former Hull and Barnsley railway, this section being used predominantly for freight. On 7 September 1964 the Monkspring Junction to Cudworth Station South Junction (the Chapeltown loop line) line closed. To allow trains to run directly through Cudworth, the section of the Chapeltown loop line, from Cudworth Station South Junction to Ardsley tunnel, was maintained, re-routed around the tunnel and connected with the existing line of the former Hull and Barnsley line to Stairfoot Station Junction, thus the former section

Stanier 8F 48113 leaves Cudworth yard in 1967.

Photograph taken from the top of Ardsley Tunnel looking across the Dearne Valley in August 1967. The view shows 8F 48169 with a Carlton – Stainforth coal train taking the new line around the tunnel heading to Stairfoot. The disconnected tracks of the old route (Hull and Barnsley) can also be seen. The new line, which used part of the old Chapeltown loop, allowed direct access to Cudworth. The Oaks Viaduct at Hoyle Mill and the Barnsley Main muck stack can be seen in the distance. (P. Hogarth)

of the line was abandoned (i.e. through Monk Bretton and Lundwood) and the track subsequently lifted.

From Stairfoot to Aldam Junction the line was predominantly level. At Aldam Junction, the electrified section from Wath Yard to Penistone on the Woodhead route was encountered. Extreme care had to be taken and if at all possible the use of fire irons, or climbing onto the tender to pull coal forward, had to be avoided. On past Mitchells Main and Darfield Main Collieries, and finally into Wath Yard if the journey was to continue after Wath, as we also undertook Mexborough Power Station jobs. After Conisborough the line started to climb to Hexthorpe Junction, where the line to Stainforth branched off to the left, then carrying on to Doncaster.

Cudworth trains to the Doncaster Decoy ended during 1966-7.

Most jobs at Royston, as previously mentioned, were for coal but we had a passenger job, the Cudworth–Leeds stopper worked with class 3 Tank Engines 40148, 40181, 40193 until spring 1962, then 4Fs worked it until being withdrawn. Before my time tanks worked the Barnsley–Cudworth–Barnsley pull-and-push service and the Barnsley–Sheffield service. We also worked the Hull to Birmingham fitted freight to Derby and later only to Rotherham Masborough; there was also a fitted freight working to Sheffield.

As previously mentioned, after passing my exam on the Friday, my first firing job was on the following Monday, with loco 4F 43906, to Roundwood sidings, not the most exciting job, but gaining experience all of the time. The best jobs at Royston were coal to Rose Grove and Manchester via the Calder Valley line. One particular job to Rose Grove was the hottest job I ever worked. My driver and I signed on at 06.40 hours, our engine being 9F 92161, and after reading the late notices and making a can of tea I climbed onto the footplate and checked the fire and water level in the boiler and tender, which were all fine. I started to build the fire, ready to ring off shed for Carlton North Siding. Dropping into a road with our train, I kept building the fire, discovering that there was no baffle plate in place, these being sometimes removed if it obstructed firing. The guard told the driver we had forty-five sixteen-ton wagons of coal and a brake van, and we were okay to move as soon as we got the signal to move onto the main line as far as Royston Junction where we then took the route towards Crigglestone, through the tunnel, over the viaduct towards Middlestown, joined the Calder Valley line, heading towards Thornhill junction, onto Heaton Lodge, through Mirfield, Elland and Sowerby Bridge. At this point the fireman's work significantly increased, the gradient gradually increasing until Hall Royd Junction and Stansfield Hall, where a banker was attached. It was then up the bank to Copy Pit, where the fireman certainly earned his money. At Copy Pit I would drop off the engine to pin

The Wath banker at Aldham Junction. Gerald Darby recalls the hazards and precautions needed when joining the electrified line with a steam train joining this section from Stairfoot. (P. Hadfield)

down some of the wagon brakes, then back on the engine, screw the tender brake hard on, and watch for the guard's signal, then proceed down the bank, the driver keeping the engine under control. At Gannow Junction the brakes were lifted and we would roll onto Rose Grove for relief. After making a brew we were then ready to work back with a train of sixty-five empty sixteen-ton wagons. The Rose Grove workings were usually undertaken also with Stanier 8Fs, WD Austerities, although I once worked this turn with a Thompson B1 61238 named *Leslie Runciman*. I enjoyed working over the Calder Valley line, and two further trips spring to mind.

First a 06.40am working to Rose Grove, with driver Charlie Sykes, our engine being WD Austerity 90345, I signed on the shed, read the late notices, went to the engine to check the water level, and started to build the fire, keeping the back corners full. I made a can of tea, followed by coming off shed down to Carlton North sidings to pick up forty-five sixteen-ton wagons of coal and the brake van. When the signal cleared, the guard gave us the go-ahead and we started to draw the train down the departure line towards Royston station. The engine did a little bit of slipping, but was a good engine. Getting the signal to join the main line, Charlie opened the regulator more to get the train moving over the junction and through the station. At Royston Junction we got the signal for the branch line to Crigglestone and Middlestown, which was a bit of a switchback [gradient] until Crigglestone tunnel, levelling out as we went over the viaduct. At Middlestown the line drops onto the Calder Valley line. The engine was working well, with plenty of steam and water, and all the way through to Copy Pit the engine continued to work well; with banker assistance, the needle stayed on the red mark, all the way to the top of the bank. We eased off, I again dropped off the engine to pin down some of the wagon brakes, and screwed our tender brake hard on, checked the water, and dropped the damper to avoid the engine blowing off. At Rose Grove we hooked off the wagons, proceeded onto the shed to coal, turn and water the engine ready to work home. We rang off shed, dropped down to the grid to pick up sixty-five sixteen-ton empty wagons back to Carlton. While previously on shed, I started to fill the firebox to the top. When I had finished all you could see was black with a flicker of flame.

When we signalled off the grid and headed to Gannow Junction, I lifted the damper and closed the firebox door, meaning no more firing of the engine was required until we reached Middlestown. On the last leg of the journey, from Middlestown to Royston the fire was still in reasonable condition, so I only added small amounts of coal to maintain steam pressure. At Royston station, I was relieved, signed off and went home. The next day we had the same job, but this time with 8F 48169. All went well to Rose Grove, onto

Visiting Britannias 70016 *Ariel* (above) and 70046 *Anzac* (minus nameplates) at Royston shed. The rundown of steam can clearly be seen in the unkempt state of *Anzac* in May 1967 compared to the smarter appearance of *Ariel*, a few years earlier. (G. Darby)

shed, coaled and watered the engine, filled the firebox, had my tea, picked up the empty wagons, lifted the damper, closed the fire hole door and off we went, with the fire burning nicely. With everything working fine, Charlie then started to ease the regulator, finally closing it and applying the brakes, being stopped at Towneley Crossing signal box. When I went to the signal box, I was informed that the previous train had failed in the section and was awaiting assistance from one of the banking engines. Our loco started blowing off, with black smoke rolling off the chimney and I was unable to keep the engine quiet. As a result we understandably got a fair bit of abuse from the local people going over the crossing. Running forty minutes late, we got right away, not before time fortunately, and we encountered no more problems on the way back to Royston.

A working trip that was exciting but scary was the one to the local Monckton Coking Plant. We would pick up empty wagons from Carlton North End Sidings to Monckton. At Monckton we would hook onto five sixteen-ton wagons to be propelled along poorly maintained coking plant sidings up the bank to the works. When the driver was given the go-ahead, we would set off like an express train, propelling the bucking and bouncing wagons towards a right and then a left-hand bend, then up the bank. Nearing the top of the bank, the regulator was slammed shut and the brakes applied, trying to make sure we stopped before the wagons finished under the coke ovens. In today's health and safety climate, this procedure would have never been allowed.

Royston's main allocation were 4Fs, 8Fs and WD austerities, however in 1962 three ex-LMS Crabs were sent to Royston, Nos 42762/70/95. These were replaced in 1963 by BR Standard 4-6-0s 73166/70/71, which were transferred and we received three Black Fives: 44912, 45207/19.

Four Ivatt 4MTs, 43076/77/78/79, replaced the 4Fs. During my time at the shed we had some interesting visiting engines:

> Royal Scot: 46106 *Gordon Highlander*
> V2: 60847 *St Peter's School York* AD 627
> A1: 60138 *Boswell*
> Britannias: 70016 *Ariel*, 70035 *Rudyard Kipling*, 70046 *Anzac*
> Battle of Britain class: 34051 *Winston Churchill*
> BR 5MT: 4-6-0 73112 *Morgan Le Fay*
> Jubilees: 45562 *Alberta* , 45647 *Sturdee*
> 9Fs, B1s and K1s

Battle of Britain 34051 *Winston Churchill* was heading towards Hellifield shed for storage prior to preservation. BR 4-6-0 73112 *Morgan Le Fay* was scrapped, this engine had no smokebox door and should have been removed at Rotherham but journeyed onto Leeds.

8F 48276 on the last official steam turn, Royston – Goole – Royston, 4 November 1967.

Footplate crew on 8F 48276, the last official steam loco turn at the end of steam, 4 November 1967. On the left fireman Gerry Harris and on the right driver Geoff Ellis.
(G. Darby)

Royston closed to steam on 4 November 1967. Operating during the last week of steam, driver Tommy Harrington and myself worked the 22.30 control order. Whatever control needed doing we did it. On the Saturday (the last day of steam) 4 November, the 14.10 Carlton to Goole was to be the very last with driver Geoff Ellis and fireman Gerry Harris on 8F 48276. Returning light engine at about 19.00, Tommy and myself signed on at 18.00 for disposal and when 48276 came on shed a vast array of detonators were exploded by the engine. The *Yorkshire Post* newspaper staff were taking photos and interviewing Geoff, Gerry, shed foreman and shed master Mr Camp. I started to clean the fire and smokebox for show only, while photographs were being taken of us. When it was time to put the engine

Photographs (below and right) taken for the *Yorkshire Post*. Fireman Gerald Darby empties smokebox ash from 8F 48276 on the evening of 4 November 1967, accompanied by Tommy Harrington (driver), although neither Gerald nor Tommy were on the footplate for the engine's final run. (G. Darby)

into the shed, No 1 Road, with a reporter on the footplate we moved off the ash pit and into the shed, and when we stopped the reporter asked for just one more ride. I said we'd just enough steam for once up and back. So we went up to the outlet and back. Then it was all over.

Towards the end of steam at Royston. An 8F locomotive is seen having ash from its smokebox and firebox removed whilst over the shed's ash pit. Meanwhile, a school party watches with interest. (G. Darby)

I left the railway on 23 December 1967, the shed finally closed altogether in 1971. I later re-joined the railway as a signalman. During my time at Royston I worked with some of the best men you could ever meet. Sadly most of them are no longer with us. I still visit the area where the shed was, but now in the main nature has taken over, yet the ash and some of the inspection pits inside the shed are still in place. The memories flood back after all these years and I can still see the lines of 8Fs, 4Fs and WDs awaiting their next turn of duty along with the drivers, firemen and shed staff.

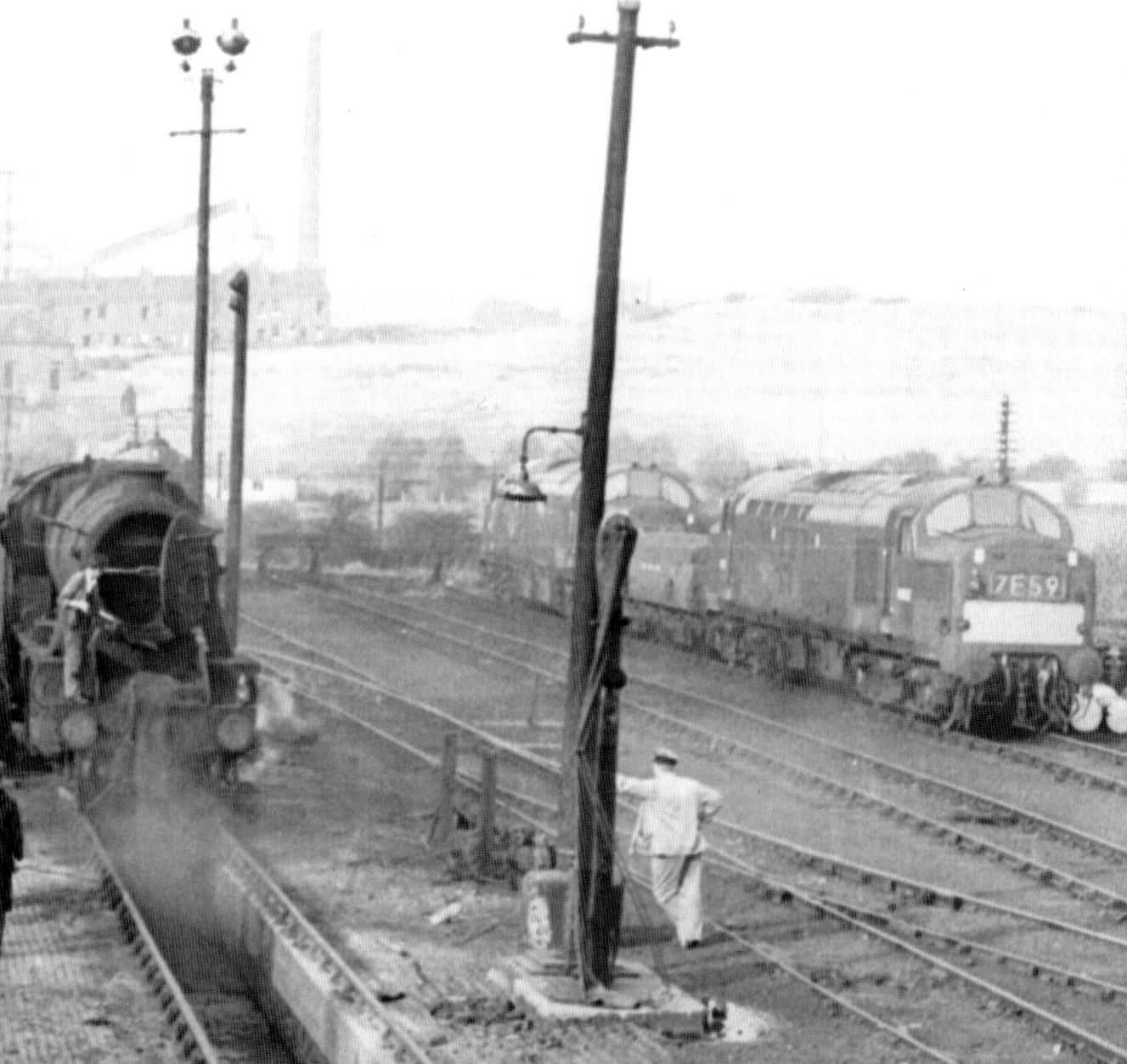

CUDWORTH STATION AND BEYOND
1950s

by Ken Gambles

WHEN I WAS 'green and easy' in the mid-1950s, it was not under the apple boughs of a Carmarthenshire farm as in Dylan Thomas's lovely poem *Fern Hill* but on a small patch of abandoned allotments just to the north of Cudworth station in the old West Riding of Yorkshire. It was, and still is, for me a magical place on which I can look back with a mixture of delight, yet sadness, that such uncomplicated, simple pleasures of one's youth can never be recaptured.

Cudworth was one of the earliest stations on the British rail network, being part of the infamous George Hudson's North Midland line from Derby to Leeds, opening in 1840. Originally named Barnsley, the station was of classical design, although passengers arriving for Barnsley had to take a horse-bus to reach the town itself some three miles away. Formally named Cudworth in 1854, the station was fully rebuilt in 1875 by the Midland

Cudworth Station as it looked in 1907.

Railway and was part of the main line from London St Pancras to the north, and following the opening of the Settle–Carlisle section, to Scotland itself. In 1923 it became part of the LMS, then British Railways in 1948, finally closing on 1 January 1968, although the line itself stayed open for another couple of decades. A belated branch line to Barnsley was eventually constructed in 1870, a part of which included the hugely impressive Oaks Viaduct which strode across the River Dearne, the Barnsley and Dearne and Dove canals and two other railway lines. Cudworth itself was notable for possessing the only stone-based signal box on the Midland Railway system. At the time I had no inkling of its uniqueness but was intrigued by its presence and would have loved to have been invited to have a look round. Sadly it was set fire to by vandals in the late 1980s as the line began to fall into decline.

My very earliest memories of our steam dominated railway system came from regular journeys from my grandparents in Cudworth to where we then lived in Grimethorpe. Not that I knew it at the time but these locos were on coal trains on the ex-Lancashire and Yorkshire Dearne Valley line serving Grimethorpe and Houghton Main collieries and were almost certainly Stanier 8Fs or WD Austerities. In 1954, aged 5, we moved to within sight of the ex-Midland main line at Cudworth and my love of railways began in earnest. Unfortunately no records survive of the next few years so I am totally reliant on memory, but those days were so vivid and played such an important part of my growing up that I am fairly sure of the accuracy of most of the following recollections.

It must have been about 1956 when I first began scribbling train numbers in a scruffy notebook by the lineside just north of the station as I can clearly remember my surprise when Cudworth North Box was demolished in that year. As one of the main lines to the north and being situated in the middle of the Yorkshire coalfield there was plenty to watch and make a note of. The staple diet in those days was a procession of full or empty coal trains in charge of 8Fs or WD Austerities (or niner aussies as we called them), 4Fs and the occasional 3F. There was much passenger activity too with regular stopping trains between Leeds and Sheffield usually in charge of ageing Compounds, Black Fives and sometimes Jubilees. The best chance for 'namers' were the London services as well as those from Bristol. In addition there were the renowned Thames-Clyde, Waverley and Devonian named expresses. These were normally in charge of Holbeck's (55A) Jubilees but locos from Nottingham (16A), Derby (17A), and Kentish Town (14B) featured regularly, as well as the stud from Bristol Barrow Road (82B). Over the years Holbeck's Jubilees became like old friends and *Queensland*, *Alberta*, *Nigeria*, *Gibraltar* and *Uganda* were almost weekly sightings. I'm sure we resorted to yelling 'Scrap it!' whenever we saw them. O the folly of youth! I've often wondered which 'Jube' I saw the most and with no way of checking I'd say *Ulster* but then again it could have been *Victoria*. Who knows? There was plenty of through freight too, with a host of 'Crabs', Black Fives and 9F 2-10-0s prominent, and in my earliest days even original Crosti-boilers. To complete the picture were the Barnsley branch trains, hauled by Royston shed's (55D) 40181, 41281, 41282 and 84009.

For the next few years I was able to indulge in my two great loves: railways and football. Through the seasons we'd gather all day on Saturday and in holidays or after school when it was light enough, playing football in the field alongside the line, breaking off whenever anything was 'pegged', before resuming our game after its passage. For a change we would sometimes create a 'slair' (a slide) down the short embankment, but overall we were left untroubled, caused no damage or nuisance and were able to revel in our pleasure. The abandoned allotments still contained some raspberry canes which added to our delight to be able to pick some fruit in the long summer holidays as well as being allowed to stay out much later in the evenings.

How different it was then. Most of my classmates at junior school went trainspotting at some time and unlike today where there is still an air of embarrassment at being a 'rail enthusiast' or 'train-spotter', it was considered a normal hobby and no-one would think to sneer at you for it. As an aside, I must have known one of my closest friends from playing football at university for about fifteen years before we both mentioned we'd been spotters in our youth and then out came the Combined Volumes for comparison.

I was pleased in those early days to see any locomotive at work (and still am) but I lacked any real wider knowledge of railways. Older lads talked of visits to Leeds, Doncaster and even Crewe where they'd seen 'Semis' and 'Prinnies' (Princesses), exotic stuff for a 9-year-old. Eventually I would venture further afield, but until I was about 10, Cudworth was the centre of my trainspotting universe.

Holidays were the best time, even in winter, for, weather permitting, we could spend hours by the lineside recording numbers. I could see the line clearly from my house but it was just too far away for me to be able to read the numbers and I'm sure we've all shared the same exasperation at seeing an engine without being able to take the number. It might have been a 'cop' but in all likelihood it was probably just *Ulster* again, yet achingly you could never be sure.

The station at Cudworth was a fine place with five ex-Midland platform faces plus another from the ex-Hull and Barnsley whose passenger service to Hull ceased in 1932. The Hull and Barnsley buildings still survived although in a dilapidated state and had been used for traffic control in the not too distant past. Our main problem was that if the stationmaster was about he used to chase us off, even though we were doing no harm, and so we developed a few subterfuges to allow us a few hallowed minutes in its confines. If he wasn't about it was alright and we wouldn't be troubled. When stopping trains were due it was possible to mingle as unobtrusively as possible with the passengers for a few minutes before departure and after the train's arrival delaying our exit as long as we dared. On cold winter days a visit to the ticket office to warm up in front of the fire was fine as long as we purchased some Toffets or some such from the vending machine therein. I can remember oh so clearly the sonorous tick from the large station clock in that waiting room. It was also possible to linger on the footbridge, which seemed to be a recognised right of way from Midland Terrace on one side of the tracks to Cudworth village on the other, on the pretext of crossing, and at times if unchallenged we would spend an hour or so gazing down into passing wagons while inhaling the smoke and steam and really being no bother whatsoever.

The enginemen were friendly and would often respond with a cheery wave to ours. A special event occurred one day when in the absence of the stationmaster we ventured onto Platform 1 to await the departure of the pull-and-push to Barnsley Court House. I have read that apparently 't' Cudderth flyer' was a nickname for the service but I certainly never heard it used. A friendly fireman noting our genuine interest asked if we would like to come up into the cab. Wouldn't we just! So three of us had that wonderful experience of seeing the blazing firebox and smelling that intoxicating mix

Cudworth 1953, platforms 1, 2, 3 and 4 (left to right).

Ivatt 2-6-2T 41281 of Royston shed with the pull-and-push Cudworth – Barnsley – Cudworth service seen at platform 3 of Cudworth station. This photograph was taken in the early/mid-1950s, before the service was terminated in June 1958.

of coal, oil and steam that is totally unforgettable. That very first 'cabbing' of 41282 is as vivid now as it was then and I'll be forever grateful for that small kindness which meant so much to a young lad.

I soon realised that a proper trainspotting book was needed to replace the old notebook I had been using and it was a proud day when my first Ian Allan publication was purchased. Unfortunately the Midland edition was underlined freehand, not meticulously underlined with a ruler, that would come as I grew older. Shortly after I graduated into the real world of spotting I went to Leeds by train with my mother and grandma, probably in 1957, and was able to see locomotives on Holbeck shed and in the station. It was very special seeing 45696 *Arethusa* on shed and a double-headed Newcastle–Liverpool service on the Leeds New Line viaduct behind 45686 *St. Vincent* and 46123 *Royal Irish Fusilier*. Strangely in the subsequent years I never saw any of those locomotives again.

One of the biggest thrills was when after much begging I was bought my very first Combined Volume, in late 1957 I think, which was pale blue and had a Southern Mogul on the front cover. It was at that moment I suppose that my railway education began. Those 'foreign' engines were immensely intriguing and their names too quite unlike anything I'd come across before,

Halls, Castles, West Countries and so on. It was also shortly after this in early 1958 that I began to realise about the mutability of life and how time changes all things, for in the two short years of watching trains, a signal box had been demolished, shed codes had changed (Leeds Holbeck from 20A to 55A for example) and the new carriage liveries introduced with the carmine and cream being replaced by maroon. Even the old 'cycling lion' symbol was replaced by a new design. By June 1958 the local service to Barnsley Court House was withdrawn and there now being no need for a connection, the 'Devonian' no longer stopped at Cudworth. Of course within another ten years steam itself would no longer be seen on British Railways.

Summer would bring a range of specials to both east and west coasts, particularly on Saturdays, and there was always the chance of a rare 'cop' or seeing a freight loco on a passenger train. Two of my friends, Alan and Dennis Woodward, had a trolley or 'bogie' or 'cart' and from very early on a Saturday morning would position themselves at the end of the long access road to the station. Holidaymakers were more than glad to have their heavy cases (no wheeled cases then) trundled along on a trolley, and being in a good mood at the start of their break would tip generously.

Sadly all my notebooks and Ian Allan books have gone to that great dustbin in the sky but I can still remember two summer workings which sent us into raptures. One Saturday afternoon heading north at speed on a special was 45672 *Anson* (then shedded at (1B) Camden I believe). But better still on another occasion during a break from our game of football Jubilee 45715 *Invincible* came powering through on a freight. Those huge Scottish numerals were always a joy for anyone from South Yorkshire and the cheering and waving in its passing was tumultuous. I can recall also at this time seeing Jubilee 45611 *Hong Kong*, which was a fairly regular sight for us, but for a time it had bright red wheels. Why, is a mystery but I'm certain it was seen on more than one occasion.

Normal fare was of course London Midland Region locomotives and I was lucky to catch the end of the famous Compounds. I recall 41066 and 40907 and how could I forget our very own Royston-shedded 40581. It was a daily sight at that time always in charge of the evening 5.25 pm (17.25) stopper from Leeds terminating at Cudworth at 6.10 pm (18.10). It was always popular, being like an old friend, and when withdrawn at Royston shed it made a very sad sight indeed on the scrapline with the sacking wrapped around its chimney.

In 1958 the Britannias arrived. They were a big talking point and my first sightings of 70053 *Moray Firth* and 70054 *Dornoch Firth* were terrifically exciting. Royal Scots too became more common on the London expresses

Jubilee 45566 *Queensland*. We saw this engine at Cudworth and the crew allowed us on the footplate much to our excitement. Neil Davenport/Online Transport Archive

with Holbeck's 46108 *Seaforth Highlander*, 46112 *Sherwood Forester*, 46113 *Cameronian* and 46145 *The Duke of Wellington's Regiment* (*West Riding*) being regular performers.

Throughout primary school I always came home for lunch. It was a penny bus-ride or could be jogged in little over ten minutes. It also provided an excellent opportunity to do some spotting and there was just time after eating to be down near the station at about 12.55 pm to witness a Bradford to London express followed by the northbound 'Waverley' before haring up Station Lane to catch a bus to get me back to school for a 1.25 pm start. In 1958 there was also about the same time a pick-up goods in charge of a 'coffee-pot' (anything that was readily identifiable was named as such) and I seem to remember 58197, 58162 or 58260 but I can't be certain.

The most memorable service of all though was the terminating 6.20 pm evening stopping train from Leeds due in Cudworth at 7.10 pm. Surprisingly this two-coach local was often in charge of main line power. I have no idea why this was so and it still remains a mystery. I can recollect 46100 *Royal Scot* featuring as well as all the Holbeck 'Scots' previously mentioned. Two particular evenings, however, stand out. Jubilee 45566 *Queensland* was the motive power and the crew after letting us on the footplate allowed us to stay on board while the two coaches were deposited in the sidings for an early train the following day. There could have been nothing more exciting than to be in the cab of an express engine moving on the main line. We were dropped at the station and *Queensland* departed north light engine. I can't thank those enginemen enough for that simple kindness providing a memory that will stay with me forever. In the 1960 working timetable, apparently this train ran empty stock to Heeley carriage sidings in Sheffield, but of the time I am writing the loco definitely worked back light engine, presumably to Leeds. The very best 'cop' on this service, however, was undoubtedly 46102 *Black Watch*, a Polmadie (66A) loco, and had there not been a number of us on Cudworth station to meet its arrival, I doubt whether we would have been believed.

There were numerous other lines in the area as a result of Barnsley's position at the heart of the Yorkshire Coalfield but the one I crossed four times a day was the western end of the Hull and Barnsley railway which crossed the Midland main line on an impressive girder bridge before descending for two miles or so to join the ex-Great Central at Stairfoot. Despite the company's grandiose aims it never actually reached Barnsley, but as one unkind commentator noted 'ended amongst spoil-heaps' to the east of the town. It was fundamentally a coal line worked in the late fifties by Stanier 8Fs, WD Austerities and Robinson-designed ex-ROD 2-8-0s whose numbers happily for me began with a 6. The house of one of my friends backed onto the line as it climbed the gradient from Stairfoot and the sight and sound of a loaded coal train slogging up the bank at walking pace and almost within touching distance was a truly remarkable and exhilarating

The Oaks Viaduct, also showing the Barnsley Coal Railway joining at Oakwell Junction, Hoyle Mill. (C. Sharp)

The Cudworth – Barnsley – Cudworth push-and-pull train crossing Oaks Viaduct in the 1950s, prior to June 1958, when the service terminated. The Coal Railway can be seen below the viaduct, with Cundy Cross in the background. (P. Hadfield)

Class C13 4-4-2T 67411 of Barnsley shed coming off Oaks Viaduct and approaching Barnsley Main Colliery, prior to June 1958. Monk Bretton Church can be seen in the top-left.

BR class 2MT 2-6-2T 84009 skirting around Barnsley Main Colliery spoil heap with the Cudworth-Barnsley-Cudworth pull and push service heading to Barnsley Court House in the 1950s prior to the service being terminated 6 June 1958. This engine was shedded at Royston and is remembered by Ken Gambles and Jeff Hodgson. P.J. Lynch

experience. Strangely I have never come across a photograph of this part of the line and sadly was unable to take photographs myself.

Bus journeys into Barnsley with my mother or grandparents afforded a first class view of the huge lattice Oaks viaduct which soared majestically above the Dearne Valley and occasionally I might be lucky and catch the two-coach pull-and-push busying itself on its way to or from Barnsley Court House station. The viaduct also crossed the canals and two branches of the old Barnsley Coal railway where ex-Great Central locos could be seen at work. In Barnsley itself, and usually before catching the bus home, I would be allowed a few minutes at Jumble Lane level-crossing from where Barnsley shed (36D) was clearly visible. Ex-Great Central motive power was dominant and I especially liked the shed's allocation of C13 and C14 classes of tank engines which worked local services to Penistone and Doncaster.

I longed to travel on the 'pull-and-push' which was so familiar to me when spotting at Cudworth but this would mean a long trek from the station as opposed to the 'trackie' (Yorkshire Traction bus) which stopped outside our house. I imagine 'pester power' might have eventually won, for one day we travelled home by the famous pull-and-push. I can almost relive that excitement and anticipation as we climbed the staircase at Court House before stepping on the wooden platform then climbing aboard for the short trip to Cudworth. The journey began on a viaduct that ran alongside Barnsley bus station, then on an embankment until we branched left by Barnsley Main Colliery, then on to the Oaks Viaduct. It was as if we were

The pull-and-push service in Barnsley Court House station, April 1950. This engine is IP 0-4-4T 58075.

flying high above the railway lines, the abandoned canals and the main road to Pontefract. We passed Cundy Cross and under the bridge on Littleworth Lane near my junior school. On the right soon came Monk Bretton Colliery, then under Burton Road bridge, past the site of Monk Bretton Station, closed in 1937, and on the left Redfearn's glassworks. Soon we were in sight of Cudworth station as we came round the South Junction curve and it was strange to see familiar places from a different perspective. There was my habitual spotting place and then we pulled to a halt and disembarked. This was the only time I travelled the route, but thankfully I managed it before closure on 6 June 1958.

On summer Sundays, weather permitting, my family, excluding Dad who never bothered, went for a long walk in the surrounding countryside. We often used to walk by Sunny Bank, or Spring Wood as we called it. Here the Chapeltown Loop, built by the Midland railway in 1899 to avoid congestion in the Rotherham area, crossed the valley on a well-proportioned viaduct. The line was still well-used in the 1950s and one service always routed this way was the up Thames–Clyde express which used to pass at about 3.10 pm on all days of the week. Quite a few times we have paused for a drink of spring water and watched as a Holbeck Jubilee with a rake of main line carriages serenely made its way south on a sunlit afternoon. Why do I remember all my childhood summers as being full of sunshine?

Close by also was an ex-Great Central single line branch to Grimethorpe

Monk Bretton station in the Midland days. The station was adjacent to Burton Road bridge and was the only one between Barnsley and Cudworth. It closed in 1937. C. Sharp

Photograph taken on 29 August 1967 from Burton Road bridge showing Stanier 8F 2-8-0 48281 of Royston shed on the former Barnsley – Cudworth route, which would have terminated beyond the colliery sidings. Monk Bretton Colliery is shown with the colliery shunter NCB Hudswell-Clarke tank No.1889, built in 1960, on the left. (P. Hogarth)

and Houghton Main Collieries which crossed the Midland at Storrs Mill, the scene of a serious crash in 1905. On Sundays there was no coal traffic and it was an opportunity to walk along the track. With grassy banks framed by hazel and birch trees it was indeed idyllic and in fact was more akin to a Great Western country branch line rather than one in a northern coal-mining area.

Spreading One's Wings

By the age of nine I was what I suppose you'd call a partly fledged train-spotter, with a regular lineside routine and a Combined Volume (still unfortunately underlined freehand, but care and precision would come with age). My knowledge of railways, their variety, shedcodes, etc continued to grow, as did an awareness of the imminent arrival of diesels. To become a 'real' train-spotter, however, I needed to be like the older lads who proudly displayed their well-kept Combines boasting of visits to Crewe, Leeds and Doncaster which filled us younger ones with envy.

Truth to tell I wasn't a particularly adventurous child, having a strong sense of danger, but also keenly aware of not getting on the wrong side of my father whose word, in typical 1950s fashion, was law. With my close

The original Royston Station was built in 1840 and was replaced in 1900. Chris Sharp

The new Royston Midland Road Station was built in 1900 and survived until 1968.
Chris Sharp

friend Alan Woodward we asked our mothers to be allowed to accompany Alan's older brother Dennis and some of the older boys on one of their day trips to Doncaster; the curt answer came that we were too young. Duly big brother Dennis returned full of excitement at his huge range of 'cops' of A4s, A1s, A2s, B16s, Shires, Hunts, Directors and so on, all exotic beasts to us novices, and we were insanely jealous. Being only nine we lacked the persuasive power, we decided to scale back our ambitions (for the time being anyway) and begged to be permitted to catch the train to Royston and Notton, the next station north of Cudworth and about two miles distant. As Alan had previously lived there and we promised not to stray too far from the station, our parents finally succumbed.

In the grander scheme of things it was small beer indeed, but as a step on the way to being grown-up and becoming independent it was a major event. I suspect it must have been a half-term holiday as it was a weekday and it wasn't in the long summer break so I would guess it would most likely have been May 1958. We were going for the afternoon only, so with a few sandwiches packed (potted meat no doubt) and a bottle of pop to share we walked down Station Lane to catch the 12.23 stopping train from Sheffield to Leeds. No longer had we furtively to avoid the stationmaster but could stroll confidently into the ticket office and waiting-room to purchase a cheap day return to Royston. Not being under the supervision of our parents made it all tremendously exciting, and whether it was because we were being trusted or that we were in charge of our own decisions, it was a memorable occasion. The train arrived, probably Jubilee-hauled 45561

Saskatchewan and 45628 *Somaliland*, which were regular performers at that time, and we were briskly transported the two miles before clambering off at Royston having avidly jotted down numbers from locos at the extensive sidings at Carlton and Royston shed itself (55D). The shed was opened by the LMS in 1932 and the company built an estate of houses for its employees at the same time. The shed closed to steam in 1967 but remained open for diesel servicing until final closure in 1971. In reality on this day it was highly unlikely we would see any locomotives we wouldn't have seen at Cudworth had we adopted our usual position, but that wasn't the point because this excursion was far more thrilling and significant.

Alan suggested a vantage point on an embankment just beyond the station and overlooking the main and goods lines. We exited the platforms, went under the line, then climbed a small bank near some houses close by Monckton Colliery and coking plant. The coke works had a huge chimney from which gas seemed to be continually burned off and was visible for miles. The colliery, where my step-grandad had worked, closed in 1968 although the coke works remained open until relatively recently. I later learnt that there was a regular coke train to Barrow and return empties to Carlton Yard which were affectionately known as the 'Barrow Babies'.

It was an idyllic afternoon: we were warm in the sunshine; well-fed and watered from our provisions; happy in indulging in our hobby; and we were free spirits. When one shared a drink from the same bottle a code was followed.

It was fine to wipe the top of the bottle with your sleeve after the person before you had had a swig, but as a mark of close friendship you had a swig without bothering to wipe the top. I'm not sure now if either was more hygienic than the other, but as a mark of being a mate (and not as painful as being blood-brothers) the etiquette was important. We must have stayed for four hours or so and although we 'copped' nothing remarkable it certainly was a meaningful afternoon in my life. I suppose by today's standards whereby 9-year-olds are killing zombies by the score or shooting gangsters on the streets of Los Angeles (on video games of course) the experience would seem utterly dull, yet it was anything but, and to travel back in time to that lovely day would be wonderful. All afternoon while we were there a small industrial loco busied itself nearby, but as it wasn't in the Combine it was readily ignored. It would be nice to think it was in fact Monckton No. 1 which is now preserved at Embsay.

On our return about five o'clock we assured our mothers that we hadn't got into any mischief and that the day had gone smoothly. Alan and I both knew, however, that this had put down a marker and that our attempts to journey even further afield would begin in earnest. Like true explorers we had already determined our next objective, not too ambitious, but one we felt definitely achievable: Normanton.

Normanton lay on the Midland main line about half an hour's travel from Cudworth and involved no change of train. Doncaster and Leeds

Normanton station.
© Rail Photoprints Collection

were still no-go areas despite frequent requests, so whether it was nagging repetition or trust I'm not sure, but along with Alan's elder brother Dennis (a mere 18 months older) we were permitted a day in Normanton. This time, being a longer journey, we did what I'm sure we've all done and stationed ourselves in the vestibule, dropped the leather straps which in those days controlled the windows, and stuck our heads out of the carriage. It was always exhilarating, if somewhat dirty, and also risky, for a piece of grit in your eye was painful and could be a trouble for the whole day. Once again Royston shed was scoured for numbers before we were into new territory (at least independently as I'd often been to Leeds with my mum and grandma). There was a stop at Walton, formerly Sandal and Walton, then across the ex-Great Northern main line from Leeds to Doncaster and the south, and the more minor ex-Lancashire and Yorkshire route from Wakefield to Pontefract and Goole, before passing the attractively-named and imposing signal box at Goose Hill Junction and running into Normanton station.

At the birth of the nation's rail system, Normanton was an important station. On the original North Midland line, later to become the Midland Railway, and before the days of restaurant cars it was a major stopping place on the long haul north. It was a designated refreshment stop and although these stops had a poor reputation for expensive food being hurriedly served before a quick departure, apparently Normanton was one of the better ones. Even when the obligatory refreshment stops ceased, Normanton remained an important station on the network.

The station itself was impressive, consisting of a very wide stone-flagged island platform with twin bays at each end. By the time of our visit it had seen better days but was still to be admired. Most importantly the staff didn't seem to mind our presence in the least and we were able to wander about at will. The advantage for us spotters was that we would get all the main line traffic that we would have seen at Cudworth but with the bonus of York to Liverpool trains plus any other services on the Calder Valley route. The line to York diverged north of the station at Altofts Junction where there was a large signal box, and the line to Wakefield diverged to the south at Goose Hill Junction. Normanton shed (55E) lay just to the north before Altofts Junction, but as we had promised not to leave the confines of the station it was tantalisingly just out of sight beyond a road bridge. There were extensive sidings in full view from the platforms and there was a fair amount of coal traffic from the nearby St John's colliery. The highlight of our day was when the Liverpool–York service pulled to a halt in charge of Jubilee 45717 *Dauntless* of Bank Hall shed (27A), a regular on these trains along with 45698 *Mars*, but they were rare locos for us. We straightaway

**Jubilee 45717 *Dauntless*.
The driver invited us up
onto the footplate.**
© David Anderson/Rail Photoprints

'name-plated' it and as we were so obviously thrilled the driver invited us up onto the footplate for a minute or so before departure. It made the day extra special but throughout our stay there was seldom a time when there was nothing to observe and of course we enjoyed seeing our regular named expresses from close up on the platform as they powered through at speed.

For a young spotter Normanton really was a fascinating place with a wide variety of traffic, being an interchange for parcels and mail, and with much to watch in the sidings alongside. There were well-proportioned Midland signal boxes north and south of the station and a glorious range of signal gantries, again of Midland origin and constructed of wood, all of which gave the feel of an important station. On a low embankment across from the platforms was one of those Hall's Distemper signs of two men carrying a plank with the name of the product written thereon. Sissons of Hull, who made the distemper, certainly hit on an excellent method of advertising and although I can say I never bought the product it was always pleasing to spot them on the lineside during one's travels. Another intriguing feature, this time on the station itself, was one of the North Eastern's tiled railway maps. Twenty-three were produced in 1903 and even by 1987 nine still survived at Beverley, Middlesbrough, Morpeth, Saltburn, Scarborough, Tynemouth, West Hartlepool, Whitby and York. We were enamoured of it and in quiet spells spent time examining it more carefully. Overall Normanton was a true pleasure with lots to see and enjoy. I did revisit in the early 1980s to take some photographs and although Goose Hill box still survived (it closed in 1990), the other signal boxes had been demolished, the station buildings were semi-derelict, the tile map had gone and where the sidings and shed used to be was just a featureless wasteland.

Another trouble-free day out had been achieved to everyone's satisfaction (we must have been well-behaved not to have disobeyed orders to stay on the station) and we were now close to attaining our main objective of a visit to a major rail centre such as Leeds or Doncaster. It was Leeds which provided the breakthrough. I suspect the logic of our parents was that it was only an extra fifteen minutes beyond Normanton, still on a direct route from Cudworth and we could be expected to stay on the station before heading home again.

And so it was that in late 1958 or early 1959 a visit to Leeds was sanctioned. Once again we had the thrill of an unescorted rail trip with windows down, heads thrust out soaking up the freedom but this time with even more in prospect. In addition to the sheds at Royston and Normanton we would also pass Stourton (55B), primarily a freight loco depot, and then the holy of holies, Leeds Holbeck (55A). I had passed the shed numerous times but on this trip the excitement really grew and the three of us yelled out names

Cudworth station and beyond   47

and numbers before comparing notes to make sure we hadn't missed anything. We were true to our word and stayed on the platforms all day. In subsequent visits there would sometimes be a purge and all spotters were

Coronation Pacific 46247 *City of Liverpool* at Leeds City station in 1961 with an RCTS special. Leeds was a favourite place for spotting although Coronation Pacifics were a rare sight at Leeds. John McCann/Online Transport Archive

cleared from the station which meant that your return ticket had to be used to regain access, hoping that this time you would be left in peace. Leeds was excellent for spotting, for not only was there a succession of services terminating or reversing, allowing us to gaze raptly at nameplates and asking 'Can we cab it mister?' but it was possible to see the motive power in the north-eastern part of the station, Leeds New, all of which in those early days were 'cops'. Having a return ticket we were able to go off the platforms into the magnificent concourse and booking area, which though commercialised still survives today and is well worth a look. There was a tea-room-cum-buffet there which had a superb huge painting on the wall of The Irish Mail headed by a Britannia, at Conway Castle I think.

Also of great interest was the printing machine which for a penny allowed you to emboss letters on a thin strip of aluminium. Girlfriends' names were very popular (Margaret Fletcher where are you now?). We had managed to see motive power at close quarters at Cudworth but there was something much more special at a busy terminus with locos being coupled and uncoupled, parcels being moved from platform to platform, and all pervaded by the smells of smoke, oil and steam. The departures were also unforgettable as locos struggled to get their trains on the move from a standing start. Leeds offered an opportunity to meet other spotters from different towns, yet we all had much in common asking what was on Holbeck, had anything decent come through before our arrival? and had anyone 'cabbed' anything? It was a long day for us but enjoyable and productive and naturally in those early years much of what we saw was a 'cop'. It might seem mundane to today's youngsters but what a treat it was on returning home to settle down with my Combine to underline (sadly still freehand) all the numbers from the day's exertions.

Now there just remained Doncaster to be visited.

Lundwood to Doncaster

This was a journey I made numerous times while I was a train-spotter, yet owing to cost and convenience it was one I made by bus.

The No. 11 Yorkshire Traction service from Barnsley to Doncaster was hourly and as it stopped outside my house, between Lundwood and Cudworth, and terminated at Doncaster station, it was ideal. I'll describe a typical day's spotting in Doncaster, which was NEVER disappointing, with a collection of memories from across the years.

With friends, usually Alan and Dennis Woodward, we caught the 8.55 bus returning at 16.00 or 17.00 depending on weather or hunger, which gave us a good few hours for collecting numbers. A return ticket cost just under two

Cudworth station and beyond 49

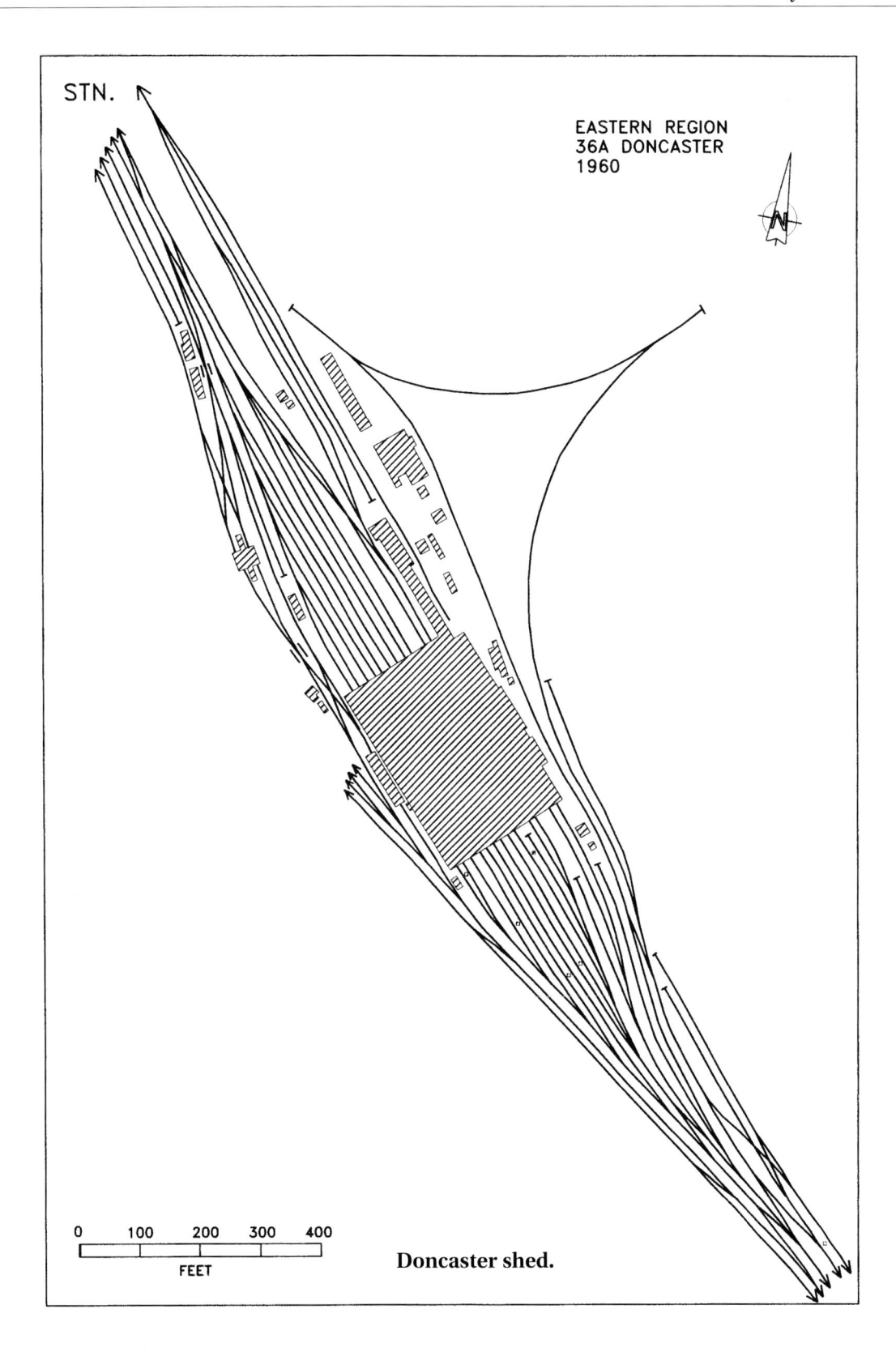

STN.

EASTERN REGION
36A DONCASTER
1960

N

0 100 200 300 400
FEET

Doncaster shed.

bob and the journey took about an hour. Once aboard, usually upstairs on the front seats, the first thing to look for was any movement on the Midland main line as we passed under Cudworth Bridges. Saturday was the preferred day of travel, but in school holidays mid-week visits were also possible. At Shafton the route turned right towards Grimethorpe and on the left could be seen the ex-Lancashire and Yorkshire Dearne Valley line where coal trains hauled by 8Fs or 'niner aussies' (WD Austerities) could regularly be seen. At South Kirby, further into the journey, there was a brief opportunity to see if there was any movement on the old Swinton and Knottingley line at Moorthorpe and occasionally we might glimpse a V2 or a B1 on a passenger duty. At South Elmsall the bus route passed the station which was on the main Leeds to Doncaster line so an express or local could be spotted. At Pickburn the ex-Hull and Barnsley branch to Sprotborough and Conisborough ran parallel to the road on an embankment but very rarely, especially on a Saturday, was there any movement.

Before too long now, with excitement building, we clambered off at the Great North Bridge, eager not to miss anything. The maroon trolley-buses adorned with Doncaster's coat-of-arms were very impressive and unlike anything we had in Barnsley, and even the destination blinds were intriguing with Balby, Beckett Road and Intake. On my very first visit to Doncaster, aged about 8, with my grandma to see relatives who ran the Dockin Hill Tavern, as we got off the bus I was thrilled to see my very first Britannia 70035 *Rudyard Kipling* powering an express on the through lines. Naively I thought it must be the Elizabethan, but later came to realise it was definitely on an East Anglia to York or Newcastle service.

Hastening down the steps by the Public Baths we raced onto the cattle dock where we would spend the next couple of hours soaking up the wonderful atmosphere. Already the dock would be lined with spotters dangling legs over the bay's edge and getting excited on hearing the chime whistle and the yell of 'Streak!' before one of Gresley's masterpieces raced through on an express, even more impressive if in charge of a rake of Pullman cars. A Doncaster resident, J6 64232, was invariably fussing about shunting in the sidings and would bring moans from time to time if it left vans obscuring our view of the main line. It was also a good place to witness trains setting off northwards after a Doncaster stop, which would often involve violent slipping and volcanic emissions as the Pacifics fought to get their trains underway and I don't think there was a more evocative and thrilling sight in the whole of my trainspotting career. Once, for some reason, 60122 *Curlew* was standing in the sidings by the cattle dock and a local lad, whose Dad apparently worked at the Plant, was loud and insistent saying, 'My dad built that!' He was bigger than us so we didn't argue.

Cudworth station and beyond 51

The Doncaster based A1 Pacific 60122 *Curlew* photographed in 1959. © Rail Photoprints Collection

The loudest cheer I ever heard there came when 60048 *Doncaster* pulled in on a southbound express; it really was remarkable and strangely I never saw the loco again. Later in the day if we made it back to the dock before catching the bus home we'd often see the 'Plantstream', four or five outshopped locomotives in pristine condition being moved onto Doncaster shed presumably for 'running-in' turns. There was always a variety of engines, some from far-off sheds, and I can recall seeing 70001 *Lord Hurcomb* and 60077 *The White Knight* both immaculate and gleaming.

After a couple of hours had elapsed since our arrival we'd begin to make our way towards Doncaster shed (36A), calling at St. James's Bridge on the way to check things out. We'd generally find out what was on standby,

Ex-P2 class 2-8-2 rebuilt with Pacific wheel arrangement. A2 4-6-2 60505 *Thane of Fife*, an engine Ken Gambles recalls seeing in the sidings adjacent to St. James's bridge, Doncaster, on one of his first visits.

invariably an A1, and see if anything was moving on the ex-South Yorkshire line which led to Barnsley and Penistone plus a connection to the Midland to allow running to Rotherham and Sheffield. On one of my very first visits, 60505 *Thane of Fife* was stationary south of the bridge in the sidings, and although many considered the Thompson rebuilds of Gresley's P2s ugly, I found them appealing, especially their most evocative names. The current P2 new build in original form, unlike these Thompson rebuilds, is to be named *Prince of Wales*.

Doncaster shed was a 'must' and my first visit was a real eye-opener, with the massive coaling tower and a profusion of engines either in steam or standing dead in lines on shed. I can recall 60113 *Great Northern*, a Thompson rebuild of a famous Gresley loco, being coaled and looking huge and powerful, and on another occasion, turning on a triangle by the shed, 60022 *Mallard*. Standing at rail level we realised just what sizable impressive machines they were and to be within touching distance of such a famous locomotive was exhilarating. Saturdays tended to be quiet on shed and so unhindered we could 'cab' the dead locos and two memories of 'cabbing' 60159 *Bonnie Dundee*, a Scottish-shedded (64B Haymarket) A1 (possibly waiting to go into the Plant), and 60002 *Sir Murrough Wilson* were unforgettable thrills.

By now it was usually time to eat and there seemed no shortage of

A4 60015 *Quicksilver* undergoing an overhaul in Doncaster Works, 1959-60. (P. Buck)

A4 60007 *Sir Nigel Gresley* in Doncaster station on the Jubilee Special run, 1959.

excellent fish and chip shops in the area. It was still a cheap, filling meal and in those days other than mushy peas and scraps/bits/batter there was none of the sausages, scampi, burgers, etc one finds today.

Our meal eaten, it was down to St James's Bridge (Hexthorpe Bridge really) to join the throngs on the walkway down to the station platform (used mainly for race-day excursions). Here you could watch as Pullman services gradually picked up speed following a Doncaster stop and marvel at the uniformed attendants, crisp white napery, silver cutlery and table lamps that were a world away from our humdrum lives. The Pullman car names were intriguing too, such as Fingall and Heron. Here the Sheffield route on the ex-South Yorkshire Railway diverged and I was lucky enough to catch the end of the 'Directors'.

Common visitors were D11s 62665 *Mons*, 62666 *Zeebrugge*, 62667 *Somme*, 62668 *Jutland*, 62669 *Ypres* and 62670 *Marne*, all shedded in Sheffield at Darnall (41A), although it was some time later before I realised the significance of their names and the connection with the First World War. I'm sure others will remember the old army tanks that used to be heaped in the Cherry Tree Lane scrapyard alongside, near to Doncaster Cold Store.

A visit to the Plant was obligatory, yet I felt it was rarely worth the effort as even by climbing the surrounding wall only the merest glimpse of a loco could be seen. It had to be done though, it was a necessary pilgrimage, but the engines I most remember were the two departmental J52s (which could be found in your Combined Edition), No.2 (68858) and No.9 (68840) which were seen through the slats in the fence by the Plant's yard. Many spotters trekked round to the back of the Plant to see the scraplines alongside the canal where at times the end of 'the Sandringhams' was visible. I only made the effort once and even then turned back half-way in order not to miss any traffic through the station. By now the day would be coming to a close and a decision made as to which bus we caught home. Almost certainly in the early days, 61250 *A. Harold Bibby*, a Doncaster resident, would have been seen, but more interestingly the W1, the Hush-Hush rebuild 60700 unique 4-6-4 which until scrapping in June 1959, was a regular on a train from Kings Cross. Our bus left from outside the station and one evening on an unattended porters' barrow were two nameplates complete with footballs from scrapped B17 'Footballers', 61664 *Liverpool* and 61666 *Nottingham Forest*. Scrapping dates suggest this must have been in the summer of 1960, but how I would have loved, and still would, one of those distinctive nameplates. I did see the 61669 *Barnsley* nameplate under the main stand at Oakwell but I don't know its whereabouts now.

My final memory concerns an evening when I was the last spotter on

A2 Pacific 60529 *Pearl Diver* at Edinburgh Haymarket. © Norman Preedy/Rail Photoprints

the cattle dock as daylight began to fade. I was able to stay so long as I was staying at my great uncle's pub for a few days. I was getting ready to set off for the Dockin Hill Tavern when the Kings Cross–Niddrie Goods steamed through at speed behind a rarity for Yorkshire spotters, 60529 *Pearl Diver*, of Haymarket shed in Edinburgh, stately and magnificent. It is a sight that will always stay with me and I'm grateful that the opportunity was there.

The journey home was usually unmemorable and then it was a case of something to eat followed by that unforgettable pleasure and excitement of underlining all the day's 'cops' in my Combined Volume. With railway-minded friends we often discuss that if we could re-live a day from the past watching trains, where and when would it be.

I'd have to say Cudworth Station in the late 1950s where so many idyllic hours were spent, but a couple of those hours on the cattle dock at Doncaster wouldn't come amiss either, and I suppose I'd have to get there on the now Stagecoach bus service, who have now acquired the Yorkshire Traction bus company.

The water tower building is all that remains of the once extensive Cudworth Station. This photograph was taken in 2015, it is now surrounded by a metal fence. The water tower can be seen in the photograph on the right to the left of the signal box.
(Barnsley & Surrounding Districts Pictorial Archive)

Journey to the Past

The most difficult and saddening journey I ever undertook was my attempt to rediscover my trainspotting past.

I had stopped trainspotting in early 1964 as the diesel takeover was most evident and, wrongly as it turned out, I could see no point in watching the final eradication of steam from the railway.

By 1979 I was married with a child and we all regularly visited my father

Peak class 45038 passes through Cudworth with a summer only 11.40hrs Newcastle to Bristol train on 16 August 1979. Ken Gambles

A view of Cudworth station in 1958 looking towards Darfield. The water tower to the left of the signal box supplied water to the pump on the left of the photograph.
R.K. Blencowe

who still lived in the house I was brought up in between Lundwood and Cudworth. One afternoon, just for old times' sake, I decided to have a stroll down Station Lane, or Midland Terrace as it was also known, to see what was left at the site of my earliest railway memories, Cudworth station. Of course much had gone but there remained some familiar signals which I had watched for years, hoping for something to be 'double-pegged'. The station buildings, minus canopies and platforms, were still in existence, as was the unique stone-based Midland railway signal box, and there were still expresses racing through in charge of Peaks and class 47s (much like in 1964). I became hooked again and determined this time to take a few photographs, which in the sixties I sadly couldn't afford to do.

Some 3,000 slides later and having witnessed the end of Deltics, Peaks and class 40s which had replaced my beloved steam, I felt vindicated that at least this time I had some physical reminders of what once was, and had confirmation that railways still held power over me. Despite the dereliction at Cudworth I took many photos, trekked out to Carlton Sidings to see a

Brush Class 47233 passes the former platform 1 buildings of Cudworth station. The station buildings were being used by permanent way gangs. The train is a late running Plymouth to Leeds service, 16 August 1979. Ken Gambles

razed colliery site, the abutments of the ex-Hull and Barnsley girder bridge which spanned the main line, and survey the desolation of the once busy yards. The 'bug' then led me to the sad remains of the once impressive Normanton station, to Leeds and to Doncaster where I had spent so many happy hours. Finding the past was obviously doomed to failure and it was a sobering experience to witness the huge changes which had occurred in

Brush Class 47527 passes Cudworth station signal box with an Edinburgh to Plymouth train, 4 January 1980. Ken Gambles

Peak class 45015 going well with a late running Summer Saturdays only Weston-Super-Mare to Leeds train, 8 August 1981. The photograph is taken from inside Cudworth station signal box. Ken Gambles

merely fifteen years. It was I suppose a kind of pilgrimage in homage to my youth and it has provided me with a record of the ever-changing railway scene. Now, almost forty years later, I'm delighted I made the effort.

The best event of all came one early evening in summer when taking photographs at Cudworth station I was beckoned up into the signal box, fulfilling a childhood dream to visit that most special place. I was able to take pictures of passing traffic and these remain some of my favourite slides. It was with immense sadness when I learned some years later that the box had been burnt down by vandals.

I didn't find the past, nor ever could I, yet I still managed to capture what little then remained and that was much better than nothing. Sadly nothing but an abandoned water tower is now left at that once wonderful scene of my childhood.

As Dylan Thomas explains in his poem *Fern Hill*, childhood can be a magical time, but of course being young we have little idea that it won't last. I am so grateful that 'Time let me play and be golden' in those lovely days of my youth. Sadly, however, the familiar people, places, sights and sounds 'are forever fled from the childless land'. What a delight it would be to be able to relive just one of those days again.

YORK STATION & VISITS TO DARLINGTON AND DONCASTER
1950s and early 1960s

by Malcolm Parker

I WAS BORN and raised near York, one of the most interesting railway venues in the UK, and I was very fortunate to have witnessed a railway scene totally dominated by steam locomotives before the diesels gradually took over in the 1960s. The station is a major junction and interchange for passengers travelling from all corners of the country. In the late '50s the ex-LNER main line from London Kings Cross to Newcastle and Edinburgh brought the Gresley Pacifics and V2s on a succession of expresses and they were joined by ex-LMS engines on trains from Bristol, Cardiff, Liverpool, Sheffield and other points to the south and west. Through trains from East Anglia added to the mix as did a host of local services to places like Harrogate, Scarborough, Hull, Doncaster and Leeds and a steady stream

Class A1 60147 *North Eastern* in York station, 1954. One of the J72 station pilots, 68677, can be seen on the right in the background.

A2 60535 *Hornet's Beauty* in York, 1954. Peter Hadfield

of freight trains. It was a marvellous place for the scores of young boys from my generation who congregated at the end of the platforms every weekend. In an era of computers, ipads and mobile phones giving young people instant access to masses of information and entertainment, they must wonder how an Ian Allan ABC book and a notebook and pen could provide so many hours of pleasure. However, whenever possible, weekends, school holidays and occasional summer evenings were spent by the side of the railway. Although many locally based engines appeared regularly, numerous other workings from distant parts of the country brought a remarkably wide range of locomotives, many of which were very unexpected having ventured far from home. Not knowing what might arrive added to the sense of anticipation – there was no means of communication to tell us what might be on the way. Although my interest eventually took me to many locations around the country, the York area was the place where my trainspotting began and where I spent most of my time. Those of us who witnessed the scene all have our memories and these are some of mine.

It's difficult to recall exactly when my interest in trains began, but I was used to seeing them pass near to home on the York–Scarborough line and my junior school in Haxby was close to the station, long since disused by passengers but still visited by a daily pick-up freight from York which shunted wagons in the yard. A B16 or maybe an ex-LMS class 2MT 2-6-0 such as 46480 busied itself with the small amount of traffic and on occasions a J27 0-6-0 such as Malton's 65844 or York's 65894 would be on duty. As I left school in the afternoon a Scarborough–Leeds express hurried through, regularly hauled by a new BR Standard Class five 4-6-0 in the series 73162-73171 when they were delivered in 1957. Other early memories further from home include the sight of the last ex-LMS Garratt 47994 leaving on a freight from York's Dringhouses yard (dad played cricket for Haxby against Uncle Tony's Dringhouses team). 47994 was withdrawn in 1958. That afternoon also gave me my first memory of an A4, 60009 *Union of South Africa*. By the age of ten I was already cycling the four or so miles over to the East Coast line near Beningbrough to watch trains hurtle past on the race track between York and Darlington. What an introduction to railways – Pacifics

A4 60005 *Sir Charles Newton* in York with an express working in the late 1950s. Peter Hadfield

Class A4 60010 *Dominion of Canada* with an early morning departure for Kings Cross from platform 3 (8s). M. Parker

roaring by on the expresses and lumbering freight engines clanking along as they struggled with their loads to and from the north-east. I was hooked and soon invested half a crown of my pocket money in the summer 1958 Eastern Ian Allan ABC. Any locos beginning with a '4' were added to the steadily increasing list ready for the day when I could afford another half a crown for a Midland book.

I took a walk around York's magnificent 1870s station recently and standing on the footbridge the memories came flooding back. The unmistakable sound of a chime whistle as the driver of an A4 gave notice he was coming through on the Elizabethan and the cry of 'streak' went up from the spotters, or an A3 struggling for adhesion on the curved rails at the north end of platform 5 (9). A huge plume of smoke, steam and cinders would shoot high into the glass roof as it shuddered on the spot with driving wheels spinning crazily and creating showers of sparks, straining to get a heavy Newcastle express on the move. Sadly there was no D49 Shire or Hunt simmering quietly in the Harrogate bay platform 8(13) – just an uninteresting DMU, albeit a brand new one. And there was no clutter of young boys on the platform ends, although I suspect some of the elderly men there were probably those very same boys of the 1950s and '60s!

It was interesting to note how things have changed. In 1958 a penny platform ticket – valid for one hour of course – would buy anything up to twelve or so hours of access, but the ticket collectors' booths and the railings protecting the platforms have long since gone along with the plethora of tangerine North Eastern Region signs. W H Smith's book store remains a reassuringly familiar sight. In the late '50s there were sixteen platforms and two through lines between the present platforms 4 and 5 for the non-stop passenger trains and some freights. Where the current platform 2 stands, there were four platforms dispatching local trains for Scarborough, Whitby and Hull (via Market Weighton). Two are now filled in for car parking spaces. At the south end, there were three more platforms where only platform 1 survives. The main line platforms are unchanged – numbers 3/4 and 5 were 8s/8n and 9 respectively, and 9, 10 and 11 were 14, 15 and 16. Two bay platforms for the Harrogate trains have now been reduced to one (no. 8) but the two southbound bays 6 and 7 (10 and 11) remain. I've used the current numbers in the text with the ones I remember in brackets. The other major track change saw the removal in 1975 of the flat double track crossing north of the station. This gave access for trains from Scarborough, Hull and the Foss Islands branch, which served Rowntree Cocoa Works and the cattle market, to platforms 9, 10 and 11 (14, 15 and 16) and the freight yards.

Looking along the footbridge and under the wonderful station clock, the original platform signal box is now a Costa Coffee. There used to be a manually operated board mounted on its southern end listing the upcoming trains and also advising platform numbers and any late running. As my travels from home were limited to an annual summer holiday at either Filey or Scarborough, names such as London, Edinburgh, Aberdeen, Bristol, Bournemouth and Liverpool conjured up images of exciting places the young 10-year-old doubted he'd ever see. How times have changed in this world of universal travel sixty years later. The board is no more, a bank of electronic screens having taken over this task. Further along platform 4 (8n), the 1906 tea rooms were converted into a staff canteen by the 1950s and later housed a relics shop and then an impressive model railway. They are now enjoying life as a licensed bar, The York Tap. Happily, notwithstanding the changes over the last sixty years the station remains fundamentally as it was, a stunning example of Victorian architecture and engineering still fit for purpose 140 years after it opened – even a cobweb of electric wires can't hide its glory!

A day's trainspotting would start early on the 6.25am York West Yorkshire bus from Haxby: 3d each way to add to the penny platform ticket. Sandwiches

The former Platform signal box above W H Smiths which now houses a Costa Coffee. The graceful curvature of the magnificent 1870s station is clear from the view looking south along platform 3/4 (formerly 8s/8n). M. Parker

were packed into my duffle bag along with my heavily thumbed Ian Allan shed book. The highly prized ABC Combined edition, priced at a massive 10 shillings and sixpence (52½p), stayed at home. The early start was to see two specific trains. The first and most interesting was the 7.15am local to Leeds from platform 1 (3), frequently hauled by a Crewe engine which we believed had arrived on a newspaper train from Manchester in the early hours. Typical of the surprises served up was a spotless rebuilt Patriot 4-6-0 45528 carrying a brand new nameplate, '*R.E.M.E.*', which hadn't yet made it to the ABC. The other early train was the first departure for Kings Cross, a four hour journey when I first caught the train in 1961, hauled by A1 Pacific 60156 *Great Central*. It now takes less than half that time. I arrived one day to find Gresley's former experimental Hush-Hush locomotive, by then converted into Doncaster based W1 4-6-4 60700, at the head of the 7.43 am departure – a streamliner without a nameplate! And a friendly driver invited me on to the massive footplate. It had a huge cab due to a wheel arrangement with two trailing axles behind the six driving wheels.

The day then settled into a familiar pattern and we took up our usual spot at the north end of Platform 5 (9), weather permitting. The platform seat just beyond the starter signal soon got full and mail and luggage trolleys were 'borrowed' for temporary perches as the gaggle of spotters built up. A series of regular departures began to arrive, an early one being the first of many named expresses, each proudly wearing their headboards. The Leeds–Glasgow North Briton train called at platform 9 (14), powered by a Neville Hill based A3, 60074 *Harvester* being a regular choice. Shortly after, we had the rare sight of Southern Region green coaches on alternate days when the through train to Bournemouth arrived from Clifton carriage sidings, except in summer when it ran from Newcastle. The station announcer recited the twelve stops before the train set off to meander slowly down the spine of the country to the south coast in eight and a half hours. In the opposite direction, a Newcastle parcels train left mid-morning from platform 10 or 11 (15 or 16) behind a Pacific, usually an A1 or A3. Much to my amazement, one of the few A3s I'd not seen, Haymarket's 60037 *Hyperion*, appeared on it one morning. The next named express was the Tees-Tyne Pullman from Newcastle to Kings Cross. Before a York stop was introduced in the early '60s, the impressive eight chocolate and cream Pullman cars dating from the 1920s would glide through non-stop at about 10.30am, carefully observing the speed restriction on the sharp curve. It was usually an A4 turn and often in the care of Kings Cross A4 60022 *Mallard*, which I must confess didn't have celebrity status for us back then. It was just another A4, and a very frequent sight.

The arrival of a through express was the signal for a frantic burst of activity. Passengers waiting to board pressed forward as mail bags and parcels were manhandled from the guard's van onto the platform and refreshment trolleys were besieged by hungry passengers on trains with no buffet or restaurant car. A wheel tapper might be heard ambling down the tracks (what price Health and Safety!) swinging his long-handled hammer and listening for the tell-tale sound of a dull thud betraying a wheel with a problem. The locomotive crew only had a few minutes to prepare the train for departure. If the engine was being changed the fireman jumped quickly down from the platform to uncouple the coaches and the vacuum brake before the loco rolled off to the shed. Engines staying with their trains were besieged by spotters and if the driver allowed we all clambered aboard, maybe even grabbing a moment on the driver's seat. It's surprising just how many young boys will fit into a Pacific cab! Tenders were replenished,

A4 Pacific 60022 *Mallard* ready to depart from Kings Cross. This engine was a regular sight at York station. © Ian Turnbull/Rail Photoprints

the fireman ensuring it was fully topped up while doing his best to avoid soaking the bevy of spotters by over-filling it. With passengers all aboard, the staff pulled on the heavy leather straps to close carriage door windows before slamming the doors shut with a heavy 'clunk'. If the engine was getting impatient the safety valve would blow, shooting steam high into the air and creating a deafening roar that had us covering our ears. A quick check of the watch and the guard blew the whistle and waved his green flag. The severe curvature of the main line platforms made it impossible for the driver to see the guard towards the rear so he listened for the penetrating sound of the starter bell positioned on a column by the start signal. The train crept slowly forward, possibly slipping several times as it advanced hesitatingly, seeking grip on greasy rails and barely gaining walking pace by the end of the platform if it was a heavy 14 or even 15 coaches. Finally the engine got on top

J72 68736 was a long standing member of York's fleet of station pilots. Towards the end if its life it was given a coat of North Eastern green and the crest of the North Eastern Railway alongside the British Railways emblem. It was later re-allocated to Gateshead depot and it is photographed at Newcastle station on 19 April 1963.
M. Parker

of its task and the train slid from view, clattering over the Scarborough line cross-over and returning the platform to peace and quiet for a while.

While all this activity was taking place on the main line there were numerous other locos scuttling around, chief among them the J72 0-6-0 station pilots including 68687, 68736 and 69016, helped on occasions by ex-LMS 'Jinties' including 47418. The drivers often had time on their hands as the locos idled between duties and they would sometimes invite us onto the rather cramped footplate. You might even get a short ride along the platform. One kind V2 driver who allowed us on board York's 60979 told us to get our heads down and proceeded to take us from the south end of platform 3 (8) out of the station and over Scarborough Bridge before depositing us back in the station. Such a small thing for them but a great memory for a young kid!

The bay platforms were in constant use throughout the day. Platform 8

With steam to spare, Jubilee class 7P 45572 *Eire* awaits departure for Bristol with an express from Newcastle. M. Parker

(13) and its former neighbour dispatched regular trains to Harrogate often behind an ageing D49 from Starbeck or York sheds, the D49/2s adorned with their brass nameplates sporting a fox above the name of a hunt. *The Fernie, The Zetland* and *The Percy* were among the familiar names – I couldn't see a class of locos being named for fox hunts today. Sadly, the Harrogate line was one of the first to succumb to diesel multiple units. The winter timetable of 1958/59 proudly boasted which trains were operated by newly-arrived DMUs – even as early as that only two daily steam-hauled passenger trains survived on the route. Platform 8 (13) holds another memory. In August 1958 the driver of a train from the north made a serious error of judgement on braking and ploughed A3 60036 *Colombo* over the buffers. I note there is a café there now – anyone there on that summer afternoon would have had a rude awakening! Meanwhile, on platform 6 or 7 (10 or 11) a Sheffield local might arrive in the care of a Millhouses Jubilee, perhaps 45576 *Bombay*, 45590 *Travancore* or 45594 *Bhopal*. The longer distance Newcastle-bound trains from Bristol, Cardiff or Liverpool would also normally trundle into the station hauled by ex-LMS locos which handed over to Pacifics or V2s. Jubilee 45572 *Eire* was a regular performer as were un-rebuilt ex-LMS Patriot 4-6-0s. The ones uppermost in my memory are 45509 *Derbyshire Yeomanry*, 45517

Far from its Glasgow home, Royal Scot 46121 *Highland Light Infantry, City of Glasgow Regiment* **heads the stock for the 11.53 to Bristol into platform 3 (8s), 13 April 1962.** M. Parker

and 45519 *Lady Godiva*. I always thought these 1930s engines in their original form had the most dated look of any engines we saw and I look forward to the appearance of *The Unknown Warrior*, a new build of the class currently under construction. Royal Scot 4-6-0s were less frequent but not unknown visitors. One that took us completely by surprise was 46121 *Highland Light Infantry, City of Glasgow Regiment* which drifted in from Clifton carriage sidings with the stock for an early afternoon York–Bristol working. Already far from its home in Polmadie (Glasgow) it was about to venture even further south.

Freight trains provided a constant diversion as they continued to roll in between the passenger services. They were a remarkable mix of wagons of all shapes and sizes in the pre-motorway era when the railways were still hauling the bulk of the nation's goods. Oil tankers, cattle wagons, open trucks, flat bed wagons, box vans, grain wagons and bogie well wagons all appeared on mixed trains. Long strings of loose coupled wagons snaked into the goods yards where many were sorted into new trains for onward journeys. Trains paused at signals accompanied by a clattering of buffers and

York Station, Darlington & Doncaster 71

Gresley's pioneer A1 Pacific 60113 *Great Northern* **from 1922 as rebuilt by Thompson in 1945, after which few traces of its origins survived. It is seen running light between platforms 9 (14) and 10 (15).** M. Parker

Peppercorn A1 60151 *Midlothian* **in York station.** M. Parker

a similar clanking of metal heralded the restart. Little attention was paid to an engine's appearance and the sight of a shining black freight loco was clear evidence that it had just been overhauled. More often it was a filthy WD 2-8-0, a Stanier 8F 2-8-0, 9F 2-10-0, B16, ex-LMS 4F 0-6-0, K1 or K3 2-6-0, O1 and O4 2-8-0 or J27 and J39 0-6-0 but V2s were also commonly employed along with Pacifics on some express services. At the rear of the trains was another long gone sight – the brake van carrying the guard, often with a curl of smoke snaking up from the chimney of his stove in the winter months.

Talk of the winter months reminds me that our trainspotting days were not always warm and sunny and twelve hours could be a long day on York station. It was a terribly draughty place in winter. When the cold became really severe, we might succumb to buying a cup of tea in the welcome warmth of the refreshment rooms on platform 9 (14), the challenge being to see how long a cup could last before we were politely asked to move on if the café was busy. Those of us that remember the winter of 1962/63 will recall that it was particularly harsh. We must have been crazy but we still went down at weekends, although there was salvation thanks to the water columns. Everything throughout the country was frozen for several weeks in the New Year but the water towers had to be kept in action so there were braziers at the foot of each column. We settled in on a commandeered mail trolley with an ample supply of coal and helped to keep the trains running by tending a roaring fire!

Returning to warmer thoughts, the line from York to the east coast resorts was extremely interesting, especially on summer weekends which brought a string of holiday trains to Scarborough and Whitby. In addition to the Leeds services, through trains were scheduled on Saturdays from Normanton, Sheffield, Bradford, Derby, Leicester and Glasgow among other places. When I had a paper delivery round that got me out of bed before 6.15 am on Saturdays in 1962, it was still common to see groups of three or four light engines coupled together heading east to haul the early morning departures back from the seaside. But interesting as Saturdays were, Sundays were often better as there were numerous excursion trains taking day-trippers for an outing. Between about 9.30 am and 12.30 pm there would be a coast-bound train every few minutes. There were many unusual workings on the annual working men's clubs and miner's welfare seaside specials, some adorned with headboards or with excursion numbers chalked on smokebox doors. Most came from the industrial West Riding or from Derbyshire or Nottinghamshire and although the majority might be hauled by Black 5s, Crabs, Jubilees, B1s and B16s the local shed masters used to commandeer all manner of engines to haul them. The only K2 2-6-0 I ever saw in York, 61742, appeared one day

York Station, Darlington & Doncaster   73

V2 60967 hurries a southbound express freight over the Scarborough branch crossover, 13 April 1962. M. Parker

Thompson B1 61361 waiting south of the station with a coast-bound excursion train. M. Parker

on a special from Sheffield to Scarborough.

At the other end of the spectrum, the Scarborough line still boasted a named train in the late '50s. Twice weekly, the summer only Scarborough Flyer paused at York to change engines as it passed from the main line to the branch. Often Pacific-hauled to and from Kings Cross, it was also frequently entrusted to a V2, while the Scarborough leg could be a D49, B1, B16 or latterly a Standard class 5 4-6-0. A single through coach for Whitby was detached in Malton where it was attached to the afternoon Pickering and Whitby train. How the North Yorkshire Moors Railway must wish that journey could still be undertaken in full today! The branch's real day of glory came in June 1961 following the wedding of the Duke of Kent and Katharine Worsley when the royal guests were conveyed back to Kings Cross from Malton hauled by A4 60028 *Walter K. Whigham*, spotlessly clean and sporting a white painted cab roof. I never thought I'd see an A4 passing through Haxby!

Around lunchtime, a further series of non-stop expresses passed through led by the morning Talisman from Edinburgh with coaching stock that included a twin-set from the pre-war Coronation streamliner. An innovation in 1960 was the Pacific-hauled Anglo-Scottish Car Carrier conveying drivers and their cars from London to Edinburgh, and in summer both the north and south bound non-stop Elizabethan expresses would run through the centre roads at about one o'clock. Thanks to their corridor tenders, they were a guaranteed A4 working and both Kings Cross and Haymarket (Edinburgh) sent an engine to Doncaster works the preceding winter to be prepared for the daily runs. Haymarket A4s rarely ventured south of Newcastle on regular services and we'd hope for perhaps *William Whitelaw, Empire of India, Merlin* or *Golden Plover*. At weekends when the Elizabethan didn't run, the engine arrived on another turn but with the headboard reversed. Shortly afterwards, the two Flying Scotsman expresses crossed north of York, passing through the station about twenty minutes apart on the centre tracks. Both would normally be Pacific-hauled but I do remember the feeling of disbelief in June 1958 when we stood open-mouthed at the south end of platform 5 (9) to witness the first main line diesel to visit York on a scheduled train as English Electric Type 4 Class 40 D201 (40 001) emerged from under Holgate Bridge on the northbound Scotsman. I had probably only ever seen photographs or drawings of diesel locomotives in the *Eagle* comic and most of those would have been North American. The variety of engines increased when the Colchester–Newcastle train drifted into platform 5 (9) generally hauled by a March Britannia. Most days it would be 70035 *Rudyard Kipling*, but we did occasionally see

Standard class 5MT 73031 waiting to take over an afternoon Bristol train arriving from Newcastle. The Derby based loco is in green livery. M. Parker

Class A2/3 60516 *Hycilla* **resting between duties on platform 2 (4).** M. Parker

Britannia Pacific, 70038 *Robin Hood*, departs from platform 6 (10) with an afternoon train to East Anglia in the early 1960s. M. Parker

others including *Robin Hood, Boadicea* or *Hereward the Wake*. Luckily I was at the station when March sent B17 4-6-0 61627 *Aske Hall* on a train from East Anglia, one of only two occasions that I saw a member of the class in York. The other time was in July 1958 when the class pioneer 61600 *Sandringham*, looking in very poor condition, arrived unexpectedly at the head of a long rake of empty stock which disappeared in the direction of Darlington. I feared both engine and carriages may have been destined for the scrapyard, although I later learned that 61600 made one last trip south to Doncaster where it was scrapped in October 1958.

A stand-by engine was positioned south of the station in the sidings leading to the former LMS Queen Street locomotive depot ready to replace any failure. Towards the end of their lives, the York based A2 rebuilds of Gresley's P2s, 60501 *Cock o' the North*, 60502 *Earl Marischal* or 60503 *Lord President*, were regulars on this task. After their demise, other A2s took over: *Steady Aim, Sun Stream, Straight Deal, Herringbone* or *Sugar Palm* were among the familiar names taking their turn along with *Silurian, Boswell, Balmoral* or *Flamboyant* from York's A1 stud. Incidentally, I have

York B1 class 61031 *Reedbuck* has received some attention from the shed staff and looks very smart as it prepares to depart for Scarborough and Whitby from platform 11 (16) with an RCTS special in May 1964. M. Parker

A 1944 rebuild of a 1920s loco, one of York's many B16s, 61454, ambles to the north shed. The B16s were employed on every type of train from pick-up freight to main line passenger on occasions. M. Parker

to say that the LNER's practice of naming many of its express locos after racehorses was not as valuable for my education as the LMS Jubilees which gave me a sound knowledge of the extent of the former British Empire. The advent of the diesels did not mean the end of the stand-by turn; in fact the unreliability of the class 40s probably meant they were called on more often than before and gave many Pacifics an extended life. Steam and diesel locos working in tandem was also a fairly common sight especially in winter when steam locos might be called on to provide train heating. And I also remember sitting in the cab of a delinquent class 55 Deltic D9002 which had been shunted into the bay platform 1 (3) in disgrace, its engine compartment flooded with oil while the stand-by took its train on to Kings Cross.

More light engine movements took place as locos from freight trains ambled round to the shed while their replacements headed to take over trains in the yards at Dringhouses or Skelton. The Dringhouses engines often went through the station on the centre roads while a long-gone curve skirting the Branches Yard connected the Up and Down freight yards with the north shed. The light engines on this line came close to the north end of platform 5 (9), giving you the chance to read a number through the grime on a work-stained cab side, perhaps aided by the shed staff if they had tried to clean the number with an oily rag. It was not unusual to be unable to tell that some locos were actually in green livery, a comment that refers equally to express engines. The first time I saw WD 90732 *Vulcan* it was the small nameplate fixed to the cab side that gave the clue as to the identity of an absolutely filthy loco. In complete contrast, on several occasions this curve provided me with some fantastic moments when Scottish based Pacifics making their way home after overhaul in Doncaster works took us totally by surprise as they came off freight trains and headed for the shed to be allocated the next duty on their way back north. I have vivid memories of A3 60096 *Papyrus* and A2 60530 *Sayajirao* with immaculate paintwork gleaming in the sunshine.

Befitting its status as a major railway town, York had a very large engine shed (see Pages 95-7 for shed layouts and allocations 1957, 1959, and 1961) with an allocation of around 150 locos in 1957, only six of which were diesel shunters. As late as 1961 over 200 engines carried the 50A shed plate, 153 of which were still steam from fifteen different classes, the overall increase in locos being largely due to new diesel arrivals including twelve class 40 main line engines. Until the early 1960s there were actually two depots as the former Midland roundhouse depot south of the station was still in use, albeit in a very sorry state with much of its roof missing. It was a base for the station pilots but sadly it was soon given over to the store of condemned

Standard class 3MT 77013 has its tender replenished in the north shed yard. The building to the right is on the site of the National Railway Museum. M. Parker

The afternoon Red Bank Parcels accelerates away on the through road between platforms 3 (8) and 5 (9) behind Jubilee 45578 *United Provinces* **and an unidentified 5MT Crab.** M. Parker

engines and it closed in 1961.

Through the late '50s/early '60s and until the class 40s arrived, York's duties on the express passenger trains and fast goods were mainly handled by the Pacifics and V2s available, but many trains were hauled by the familiar workhorses from the B1 and B16 classes. York had always had a large B16 allocation and there were still thirty-eight in service in 1961, working on all types of train. Despite the arrival of 08 diesels in 1956/7, there were still thirteen 0-6-0 steam shunters in 1961, the ex-LNER classes being augmented by a number of ex-LMS 'Jinties'. The erosion of the older steam classes was steadily gaining momentum however. Only one of the seven D49s based at York in 1957 survived until 1959 and the few locos from the D20, J71, J77 and T1 classes all fell victim to the cutters torch before 1961. In addition to the 'Jinty' shunters, several other ex-LMS classes added to the mix in the early '60s but there were very few of the new Standard classes with only ten WD 2-8-0s and a lone 3MT 2-6-0 by 1961. The brand new 5MT 4-6-0s that arrived in 1957 soon headed off to bases in the West Riding.

The main depot north of the station was a very substantial operation. Most of the shed has found a new lease of life as the National Railway Museum, greatly modified and with only one of its original four turntables. Its current condition is also in stark contrast to the gloomy smoke-filled interior of its working life, when the darkness was penetrated on bright days by shafts of sunlight piercing gaps in the roof. Deft footwork was needed to avoid the puddles of rainwater and oil on the floor. When the station quietened a little in the early afternoon we would walk down Leeman Road to see what engines were visible. North Eastern Crescent, a row of railway cottages, ran down in an arc from Leeman Road close to the original museum entrance which closed in 2019. It led to a gate overlooking the yard where engines were idling in the open between duties, having ash pans emptied or tenders topped up. A track ran northwards from the gate and it was possible to check what was about, keeping a wary eye out for railway staff although they rarely bothered us. Most of the yard area now lies under the Siemens servicing depot. Further along Leeman Road engines stood under the massive concrete coaling tower or waited to be spun on the turntable. As the 1960s progressed the sidings by the turntable became a stabling point for diesel engines between duties. The loco depot was particularly impressive on Sundays when around two hundred engines would normally be on shed, simmering away quietly under a pall of acrid green sulphurous smoke. It's difficult to imagine what the living conditions were like for the inhabitants of the railway cottages.

Back at the station after our visit to the shed the activity continued

Freshly out-shopped A4 60013 *Dominion of New Zealand* backs off platform 7(10) where it has just arrived in ex-works condition with a train from Doncaster. M. Parker

Class A4 60015 *Quicksilver* glides through the station with a south bound express. M. Parker

unabated. What we called the 'Red Bank Parcels' was a lengthy double-headed train with over twenty vans which took two engines over to Manchester in the early afternoon. I think it was actually empty newspaper vans being returned over the Pennines and it was interesting for the combinations of Jubilees, Black 5s or Crabs that would be in charge. The afternoon expresses kept rolling in from all directions. The two Pacific hauled Northumbrians running between Kings Cross and Newcastle called at the station and there was also a boat train, the Norseman, which operated in the summer months between London and the Tyne Commission Quay at Newcastle where it connected with the Bergen ferry. Around half past four the Heart of Midlothian to Edinburgh paused on platform 5 (9). After a Liverpool–Newcastle express called at about 6 pm, the non-stop afternoon Kings Cross–Newcastle Talisman passed through on the middle road at about 7pm. With the day beginning to draw to a close, a train of refrigerated white vans laden with fish hurried south on the centre road at the maximum permitted speed, usually in the care of a 9F 2-10-0. It originated in Aberdeen and was timed for an early morning arrival in the capital to get the fish to Billingsgate market. Our last chance of an interesting ex-LMS loco came with the arrival of a Bristol–York train due at about 7.45 pm, hopefully a Royal Scot. Finally, if it was on time, during the week our day ended with the 8 pm arrival of the north bound Tees-Tyne Pullman which we might see before dashing out to catch the five past eight bus home.

Back in Haxby, the day ended with recording the new engines in the ABC Combine, working through the columns of numbers scribbled in the note book. Although some locomotives did stray far from home in the late '50s/early '60s, there were more regional characteristics than is the case today. It was many years before I saw steam locomotives with an ex-Great Western copper cap chimney or a former Southern loco beginning with a '3'. You had to travel considerable distances from York to find such treasures, confined as they were to the west and south of the country. We did, however, have tremendous variety on our doorstep. On a typical day we could expect all four types of East Coast Pacific, V2s, B1s, B16s, D49s, K1s, K3s, O1s, O2s, O4s, J27s, J94s, J72s, Britannias and other Standard classes 2, 4 and 5, WD 2-8-0s and 9Fs not to mention various ex-LMS Fairburn or Fowler tank locos, 6P5F 'Crabs', 3Fs, 4Fs, Stanier Black 5s, Jubilees, Patriots, the occasional Royal Scot and a steady stream of Stanier 8Fs. It was an incredibly diverse range of motive power, in contrast to today's handful of diesel and electric loco classes and numerous diesel and electric units. In addition to variety, we were also very fortunate with the sheer number of engines seen during a normal day. York only has the Siemens maintenance depot today with few locomotives on view – what a contrast to the sights we enjoyed in the days of the steam powered railway!

Although I began my spotting days on a totally steam operated railway, the change to diesel power altered the scene quickly over the first years of the 1960s. When D201 appeared in 1958 it marked the beginning of rapidly accelerating, inexorable change, although York shed hung onto its last few steam locos until as late as June 1967. Apart from a handful of 08 shunters and the first DMUs, there were no diesels to be seen before 1958. All too soon the Britannias stopped arriving from East Anglia, replaced by early class 31s and 37s. On the East Coast main line the class 40s were joined by class 45 and 46 Peaks, 47s and then the powerful class 55 Deltics in 1961, capable of emitting a roar and a cloud of diesel exhaust when accelerating that excited some spotters as much as any chime whistle – but not me. Freight trains from the north-east arrived behind Thornaby class 25s, 27s or 37s, often aided by brake tenders to help keep the loose-coupled wagons in check. And new long distance workings brought pairs of Southern-based class 33s in 1961 on the daily Blue Circle cement train from Cliffe to Uddingston. Local trains to Harrogate, Scarborough and Leeds were all handed over to diesel multiple units, and some services, including the direct trains to Hull via Market Weighton, were cut completely in 1965 as the effects of the Beeching Report were felt. Local pick-up freights also disappeared. The smoke no longer hangs over Leeman Road and many diesels have in turn been replaced by electric traction on the East Coast main line. I've always maintained an interest and pause to watch passing trains wherever I may see them, although I've long since stopped spending endless hours waiting patiently by the track side to see what might arrive. But I'm just so grateful that by chance I was able to witness the never-to-be-repeated scene that was the steam dominated railway in late '50s/early '60s York. A truly wonderful and unforgettable time.

Darlington and Doncaster

I moved to a York-based secondary school in 1959 and was lucky enough to find an active railway society that over the next few years took me to over 120 sheds and several loco works around the country. My first trips were to Darlington and Doncaster, both easily accessible from York and acceptable to my parents as we had a teacher travelling with us. We also had pre-arranged permits for most depots so there was to be no hiding

A clear sign of recent overhaul: newly out-shopped locos in pristine condition on Darlington shed. Above: V2 60857, 28 October 1959. Below: Tyne Dock-based Class 9F 2-10-0 92098, 2 June 1962. M. Parker

Class J27 0-6-0 65822 from Blyth depot, 2 June 1962. M. Parker

from shed foremen or darting between locos to avoid detection. In truth the rail journey to neither is very exciting from York but at least it got us on the main line with a chance to travel on some of the expresses we'd been watching at the station.

Wasting little time, the first trip was to Darlington in October 1959, one of four visits between then and 1962. Travelling north on a Birmingham–Newcastle express we shot by my lineside vantage point at Beningbrough on the famous race track where the pioneer HST was to set the world speed record for diesels of 143mph in 1973. Northallerton was the only loco shed between York and Darlington but unless it was providing a temporary home to an engine that had failed on the main line it was hardly a scene of interest or great activity. I went round it in December 1962 when there were just two locos present, Standard class 2 2-6-0 78010, which was one of six class members allocated there, and WD 2-8-0 90072 which had doubtless failed on a freight train.

Pulling into Darlington, trains veer from the main line enabling through expresses to continue unhindered at high speed. I recall there being two locomotives from the Stockton and Darlington Railway mounted on plinths in the station, *Locomotion No 1* and No 25 *Derwent,* both of which are now housed in Darlington North Road Museum. The East Coast expresses were the trains with which we were familiar from our trips to York and as the local

The end of the road for Thornton based D49/1 62728 *Cheshire* as it waits in Darlington shed yard before transferring to the works for scrapping, 28 October 1959. M. Parker

branch services to Bishop Auckland and Stockton were in the hands of DMUs it was not the most exciting station if you were in search of new locos. There were however interesting engines to be found in the town thanks mainly to the engine works and our trips normally included visits both there and to the shed. The sheds were dominated by freight locos although there would normally be a few Pacifics, one of which stood on stand-by duties for the main line. Of greater interest were locomotives either waiting to go into the works looking rather neglected or gleaming in their new coat of paint as they waited to go home. The main interest for us were the few Scottish-based engines that were sent south for servicing. Scottish V2s were particularly sought after and I have notes of 60823, 60825, 60953 (all St Margarets Edinburgh), 60920 (Dundee), 60927 (Haymarket) and 60955 (Aberdeen) in 1959. On my first

York Station, Darlington & Doncaster **87**

Two Yorkshire based locos, Millhouses shed Class 2MT 46451 ahead of Mirfield's B1 61040 *Roedeer,* 2 June 1962. M. Parker

WD 2-8-0 90451 is still bright and shiny after a short trip from Darlington to its home shed at Thornaby on 2 June 1962. M. Parker

visit there were also two Scottish V1s and a V3 from Eastfield (Glasgow) or one of its sub-sheds. I recall one of these having the equipment for acting as a banker on trains tackling the steep gradient out of Glasgow Queen Street. York had been an excellent place to see the rapidly disappearing D49s but over twenty were based in Scotland or Carlisle and I was very pleased to see 62728 *Cheshire* from Thornton shed and 62734 *Cumberland* from Carlisle Canal returning to where they had been built in the late 1920s on visits in 1959 and 1961. As I mentioned earlier, freight locos dominated the scene in the industrial north-east and a few classes were very well represented. The Q6s and Q7s come to mind and, along with numerous J27s, there were also J25s and J26s. A few one-offs occurred as well including a 4-8-0T T1 69921, a diminutive 0-4-0 Y1 68149, a Thornton based 0-6-0 J6 64477 and the last 0-6-0 J21 65033 which was awaiting its fate on the shed in December 1962. It was one of the comparatively few engines which had a reprieve and a happy ending. Inevitably, the number of diesel locos increased rapidly in the early '60s and the works were also building new engines including 08 shunters and class 25 Bo-Bos. Despite this, Darlington still had a significant number of steam locos in June 1962 when 64 of the 76 engines listed on a shed visit were steam as were 65 of the 96 locos on the works, and half of the diesels were 08 shunters under construction. Interestingly there were no fewer than fifty-five DMU coaches made up into 2, 3 and 4 car sets in the diesel depot. Loco numbers seemed to be declining steadily however as a visit later in the year had only 40 engines on shed (35 steam) and 69 on the works (38 steam).

The second school trip took me in the opposite direction along the main line to Doncaster, another railway town with a major locomotive works as well as a busy running shed. As it was so convenient, we visited five times between February 1960 and April 1963, going round the works on four of these. The earlier tours were done by rail but sadly we found a diesel waiting to carry us south in 1960, although my favourite 7.15 am to Leeds didn't let me down and the day got off to a good start thanks to the sight of Crewe's Royal Scot 46135 *The East Lancashire Regiment* waiting to depart for Leeds from the bay platform. Our route to Doncaster took us along the original North Eastern Railway tracks built in 1871 but closed when the line was diverted around the Selby coalfield in 1983. Much of it north of Selby is now converted to a cycle way forming part of the Trans Pennine Trail and the remainder is used by an improved A19 road. Leaving York station, the main line went past Dringhouses yard where there was sure to be activity as one of the first 08 shunters allocated to York assembled trains for onward movement. On the outskirts of the city, the line turned off to the south-west at Chaloners Whin Junction, close to where

A class 55 Deltic pulling away from the speed restriction over Selby swing bridge with the 0800 Edinburgh-Kings Cross express. M. Parker

the park-and-ride facility has now been built. The route was fairly uneventful and good for decent timings apart from problems caused by river crossings over the Ouse at Naburn and Selby. Both had swing bridges topped with central cabins erected over the tracks for the bridge operatives although the Naburn bridge did not open for river traffic after 1956. Speed restrictions were imposed on both bridges and the Selby area had the added disadvantage of severe curves which British Rail must have been delighted to eliminate when the 1983 diversion opened.

   Arriving into Doncaster, we would settle in for some spotting before our visits to the shed and works. The station is an excellent place to watch expresses at speed as any non-stop trains can take advantage of the flat straight track to storm through the middle roads unobstructed. The Pacifics looked extremely impressive as they hurtled through hard at work. As with York, much freight misses the station thanks to avoiding lines but there was still a steady stream of movements to keep us occupied. It may seem odd as York is so close to Leeds but some of the Pacifics that were hardest for us to see were the A1s allocated to Copley Hill for the expresses between the West Riding and Kings Cross. I was delighted to finally see 60117 *Bois Roussel*, 60118 *Archibald Sturrock*, 60120 *Kittiwake* and 60131 *Osprey* on some of my early trips. The first visit I made to the sheds on Doncaster Carr set the tone for all later trips with a great variety of freight and shunting locos: B1s, K3s, O2s, O4s, J39s, J50s, J69s, J72s, J94s and WD 2-8-0s were all represented. Doncaster was surrounded by countless active collieries

Class A3 60063 *Isinglass* in Doncaster, fresh from overhaul and fitted with German-style smoke deflectors, 2 January 1962. M. Parker

generating millions of tons of freight traffic and the memory of long rows of coal trucks lumbering along behind clanking 2-8-0s from WD, O1, O2 or O4 classes is still very strong. As with Darlington, what often made the sheds interesting were the locos either waiting to go to the works or recently released. Doncaster was the main works for servicing the East Coast Pacifics from the entire route which meant the Scottish engines made the trip south. The first sight that often greeted you on arrival at the shed would be a 4-6-2 from north of the border awaiting its turn. In 1960 I arrived to find A1 60162 *Saint Johnstoun* looking forlorn and in need of attention and later in the works A2 60529 *Pearl Diver* was already dismantled and under repair. The works were still steam dominated and three Britannias were among the engines receiving attention, Doncaster having the job of overhauling these from all regions. 70002 *Geoffrey Chaucer* and 70013 *Oliver Cromwell* from the Eastern Region were joined by 70014 *Iron Duke*, a Stewarts Lane engine whose duties included the Golden Arrow. Less fortunate were three B17s, 61618 *Wynyard Park*, 61658 *The Essex Regiment* and 61663 *Everton,* which I don't think were destined to leave in one piece. Doncaster was also given the task of scrapping some ex-LMS locos and the B17s were accompanied by 2P 40582, 3Fs 43665 and 43759 and a 3MT, 40025. The works were building electric locomotives for the Southern Region with E5017-E5021 in various stages of construction. Only two of them lasted long enough to receive TOPS numbers as 71003 (E3018) and 71005 (E5020) although even these were withdrawn in 1977. In addition, Doncaster received newly-built diesels for

Newly arrived from its English Electric manufacturers, Class 40 diesel D261 (later 40061), the first of seven allocated to Haymarket depot, in Doncaster Works yard, 29 February 1960. M. Parker

acceptance before they were released into traffic and English Electric Type 4 D261 (40 261) had arrived from the Newton-le-Willows works. A4 60022 *Mallard* was in the works and we speculated that this Kings Cross engine was probably being prepared for the Elizabethan in the coming summer. We did have the opportunity to squeeze through the corridor tender and I suspect there may have been some, shall we say more portly drivers, who had to be excused from this duty.

When I returned in 1961 there were forty-one locos on the shed and not a diesel in sight. The Scottish Pacific waiting for the works was A3 60098 *Spion Kop* but the remainder of the engines were freight or mixed traffic locos, the most powerful being seven V2s and the rest including B1s, K1s, K3s, O2s, O4s, one of which was the now preserved 63601, L1s, an ex-LMS 4MT, a Stanier 8F and WD 2-8-0s. The works were also still busy with steam overhauls, 42 of the 67 engines being steam. I wasn't disappointed by the Scottish Pacifics seen as they included my last A4, 60024 *Kingfisher* along with an A3 60099 *Call Boy* and an A2 60525 *A.H. Peppercorn*. Perhaps the most interesting loco of the day however was K1 61997 *MacCallin Mor*, far

Haymarket A3 Pacific 60094 *Colorado* stands at the tunnel end of Glasgow Queen Street, having worked in on a service from Edinburgh, 1950. Haymarket were still sending its Pacifics to Doncaster for attention when I saw this engine in 1962. © Rail Photoprints Collection

from its home on the West Highland line. On this visit two Eastern Region Britannias, 70001 *Lord Hurcomb* and 70005 *John Milton*, were accompanied by two from the Western Region: 70023 *Venus* and 70027 *Rising Star*. The early problems encountered by the Deltic diesels were evident as two of them, D9004 and D9005 (55004 and 55005), were already back in for attention. As keen railway enthusiasts we even went round the carriage works but it was interesting as we saw a former first class twin-set from the 1937 Coronation being prepared for the royal wedding of the Duke of Kent later in the year.

My first Sunday visit to the shed was in 1962 when there were eighty-four locos on shed and only seven diesels were present, six of which were 08 shunters. The sole class 37, D6737 (37037), must have looked completely out of place. A healthy group of A1, A2 and A3 Pacifics were still active including the much-abused Gresley pioneer 60113 *Great Northern*. The first Britannia, 70000, *Britannia* herself was joined by classmates 70007 *Coeur-de-Lion* and

70012 *John of Gaunt*. Other classes included Stanier 8Fs, WD 2-8-0s, B1s, K1s, J50s, O2s, O4s, 9Fs, V2s, and single representatives from Standard 2MT, ex-LMS 4MT, 3F Jinty and Stanier 8F. A wonderful cocktail of motive power! At the end of December the same year we saw fewer locos on shed, only fifty-seven, but it was a Monday rather than a Sunday. Haymarket was still sending its Pacifics south for attention and 60094 *Colorado* was waiting its turn – I hope it was overhaul and not the cutter's torch. Diesels were still sparse on shed with three 08 shunters and one other non-steam loco, but interestingly this was the first Brush class 47 D1500 (47401). The decline of steam was more evident on the works which actually ended steam overhauls the following year. *Colorado's* hopes of survival looked quite good as there were two more Scottish Pacifics under repair, 60041 *Salmon Trout* and 60090 *Grand Parade*, the latter being great news for me as it was the last of the class I saw. But of 52 engines in the works only 18 were steam. The other steam engines deemed worthy of attention were members of K1, B1, WD 2-8-0 and V2 classes. Manufacture of electric locos for the West Coast continued with E3089-E3094 (85034-85039) in various stages of completion.

I'm pleased that my last visit to Doncaster Carr was on a Sunday early in April 1963. Looking at the list now, I am surprised that steam power

60090 *Grand Parade* at Haymarket, 1962. This was the last of its class I ever saw. © Rail Photoprints Collection

A4 Pacific 60017 *Silver Fox* at Doncaster in 1962. © Rail Photoprints Collection

remained utterly in control. The collieries were all still in operation and consequently the demand for rail haulage from the pits to the power stations was in full swing. As always, freight locos predominated, but there were several Pacifics resting between duties: A3s 60039 *Sandwich*, A1s 60114 *W.P. Allen*, 60118 *Archibald Sturrock*, 60149 *Amadis*, 60155 *Borderer*, 60157 *Great Eastern*, 60158 *Aberdonian*. For the first time there were no Scottish Pacifics either heading for the works or heading home after their release. I fear that A4 60017 *Silver Fox* might have been heading on its final short journey to the works. The 107 engines on shed were the most I ever saw in a single visit to 36A and only eleven were diesels, three 08s, an 03, four class 37s, two class 40s and a sole class 47. It was a fitting end to my memories of Doncaster as we boarded our coach and headed for the other eleven sheds in Derbyshire and Nottinghamshire on the list that day!

**NER REGION
50A YORK
1959**

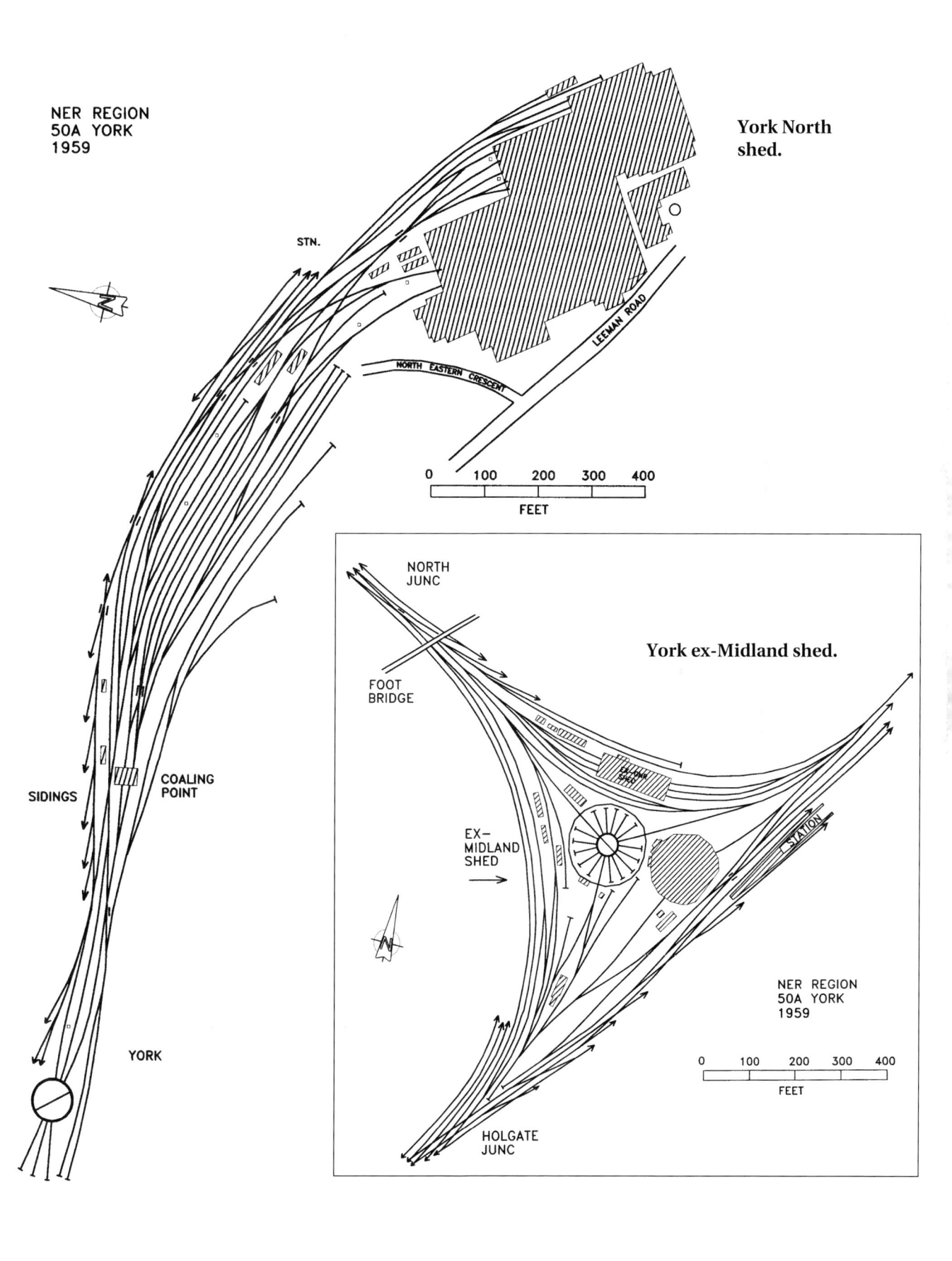

STN.

York North shed.

NORTH EASTERN CRESCENT

LEEMAN ROAD

0 100 200 300 400
FEET

SIDINGS

COALING POINT

YORK

NORTH JUNC

FOOT BRIDGE

York ex-Midland shed.

EX-MIDLAND SHED

EX-YORK SHED

STATION

**NER REGION
50A YORK
1959**

0 100 200 300 400
FEET

HOLGATE JUNC

YORK MPD ALLOCATION 1957
As at May 11th 1957

13237, 13238, 13239, 13240, 13313, 13314, 13315, 13318, 13319, 13320 Later re-numbered D3237, etc and allocated 08 series numbers under the TOPS system

13237:08169, 13238:08170, 13239:08171, 13240:08172, 13313:08243, 13314:08244, 13315:08245, 13318:08248, 13319:08249, 13320:08250

Class A1 4-6-2
60121 *Silurian*, 60138 *Boswell*, 60140 *Balmoral*, 60146 *Peregrine*, 60153 *Flamboyant*

Class A2 4-6-2
60501 *Cock o' the North*, 60502 *Earl Marischal*, 60503 *Lord President*, 60512 *Steady Aim*, 60515 *Sun Stream*, 60522 *Straight Deal*, 60524 *Herringbone*, 60526 *Sugar Palm*

Class V2 2-6-2
60837, 60839, 60843, 60847 *St Peter's School, York*, AD 627, 60856, 60864, 60895, 60904, 60907, 60918, 60925, 60929, 60934, 60941, 60946, 60954, 60960, 60961, 60963, 60968, 60974, 60975, 60976, 60977, 60981, 60982

Class B1 4-6-0
61002 *Impala*, 61016 *Inyala*, 61017 *Bushbuck*, 61038 *Blacktail*, 61053, 61071, 61084, 61115, 61288, 61337, 61339

Class B16 4-6-0
61416, 61417, 61418, 61419, 61420, 61421, 61422, 61423, 61424, 61426, 61430, 61434, 61435, 61436, 61437, 61438, 61439, 61441, 61443, 61444, 61448, 61449, 61450, 61452, 61454, 61455, 61457, 61459, 61460, 61461, 61462, 61463, 61464, 61465, 61466, 61467, 61468, 61472, 61473, 61475, 61476, 61477

Class K1 2-6-0
62046, 62047, 62048, 62049, 62050, 62056, 62057, 62061, 62062, 62063

Class D20 4-4-0
62395

Class D49/1
62702 *Oxfordshire*, 62730 *Berkshire*, 62731 *Selkirkshire*

Class D49/2
62745 *The Hurworth*, 62747 *The Percy*, 62760 *The Cotswold*, 62771 *The Rufford*

Class J25 0-6-0
65685, 65691, 65714

Class J27 0-6-0
65793, 65845, 65857, 65874, 65883, 65887, 65890, 65894

Class J94 0-6-0ST
68029, 68031, 68032, 68040, 68042, 68044, 68046, 68061

Class J71 0-6-0T
68246, 68250

Class J77 0-6-0T
68435

Class J72 0-6-0T
68677, 68686, 68722, 68724, 68726, 68735, 68739, 69020

Class T1 4-8-0T
69910, 69913, 69916

Class 5MT 4-6-0
73162, 73163, 73164, 73165, 73166, 73167, 73168, 73169

TOTAL: 161

08 Diesel 10, A1 5, A2 8, V2 26, B1 11, B16 42, KI 10, D20 1, D49/1 3, D49/2 4, J25 3, J27 8, J94 8, J71 2, J77 1, J72 8, TI 3, 5MT 8

YORK MPD ALLOCATION 1959
As at April 11th 1959

D3237, D3238, D3239, D3240, D3313, D3314, D3315, D3318, D3319, D3320
2MT 2-6-2T, 41252
4MT 2-6-4T, 42083, 42085
2MT 2-6-0, 46480, 46481
3F 0-6-0T, 47239, 47254, 47334, 47403, 47418, 47421, 47436, 47448, 47556, 47607

Class A1 4-6-2
60121 *Silurian*, 60138 *Boswell*, 60140 *Balmoral*, 60146 *Peregrine*, 60153 *Flamboyant*

Class A2 4-6-2
60501 *Cock o' the North*, 60502 *Earl Marischal*, 60503 *Lord President*, 60512 *Steady Aim*, 60515 *Sun Stream* 60522 *Straight Deal*, 60524 *Herringbone*, 60526 *Sugar Palm*

Class V2 2-6-2
60828, 60837, 60839, 60847 *St Peter's School, York*, AD 627, 60855, 60856, 60864, 60876, 60877, 60878, 60887, 60895, 60907, 60918, 60925, 60939, 60941, 60946, 60954, 60960, 60961, 60963, 60968, 60974, 60975, 60977, 60981, 60982

Class B1 4-6-0
61002 *Impala*, 61053, 61069, 61071, 61084, 61086, 61288, 61337

Class B16 4-6-0
61410, 61413, 61416, 61417, 61418, 61419, 61420, 61421, 61422, 61423, 61424, 61426, 61430, 61434, 61435, 61436, 61437, 61438, 61439, 61440, 61441, 61443, 61444, 61448, 61449, 61450, 61451, 61452, 61453, 61454, 61455, 61457, 61460, 61461, 61462, 61463, 61464, 61465, 61467, 61468, 61472, 61473, 61475, 61476, 61477

Class K1 2-6-0
62046, 62048, 62049, 62050, 62056, 62057, 62061, 62062, 62063,

Class D49/2
62740 *The Bedale*

Class J25 0-6-0
65698, 65714

Class J27 0-6-0
65845, 65874, 65883, 65887, 65890, 65894

Class J94 0-6-0ST
68032, 68040, 68046, 68061

Class J71 0-6-0T
68309

Class J77 0-6-0T
68392, 68431

Class J72 0-6-0T
68677, 68687, 68736, 69016, 69020

3MT 2-6-0
77012

WD 2-8-0
90068, 90200, 90230, 90236, 90405, 90424, 90445, 90475, 90543, 90578

TOTAL: 160

08 Diesel 10, 2MT 1, 4MT 2, 2MT 2, 3F 10, A1 5, A2 8, V2 28, B1 8, B16 45, K1 9, D49/2 1, J25 2, J27 6, J94 4, J71 1, J77 2, J72 5, 3MT 1, WD 10

YORK MPD ALLOCATION 1961
As at 10th June 1961

4MT 2-6-4T
42085, 42553

4MT 2-6-0
43014, 43055, 43056, 43071, 43096

2MT 4-6-0
46480, 46481

3F 0-6-0
47239, 47421, 47448, 47556

A1 4-6-2
60121 *Silurian*, 60138 *Boswell*, 60140 *Balmoral*, 60146 *Peregrine*, 60150 *Willbrook*, 60153 *Flamboyant*, 60154 *Bon Accord*

A2 4-6-2
60502 *Earl Marischal*, 60512 *Steady Aim*, 60515 *Sun Stream*, 60516 *Hycilla*, 60518 *Tehran*, 60522 *Straight Deal*, 60524 *Herringbone*, 60526 *Sugar Palm*

V2 2-6-2
60810, 60828, 60831, 60837, 60839, 60842, 60847 *St Peter's School York A.D. 627*, 60855, 60856, 60864, 60876, 60877, 60878, 60879, 60887, 60895, 60907, 60918, 60925, 60939, 60941, 60954, 60961, 60963, 60968, 60974, 60975 60977, 60981, 60982

B1 4-6-0
61002 *Impala*, 61018 *Kudu*, 61020 *Gemsbok*, 61021 *Reitbok*, 61031 *Reedbuck*, 61039 *Steinbok*, 61049, 61053, 61062, 61068, 61069, 61071, 61084, 61086, 61198, 61229, 61240 *Harry Hinchcliffe*, 61273, 61276, 61288, 61291, 61319, 61337, 61388

B16 4-6-0
61417, 61418, 61419, 61420, 61421, 61422, 61423, 61425, 61431, 61434, 61435, 61436, 61437, 61438, 61439, 61443, 61444, 61448, 61449, 61450, 61451, 61452, 61453, 61454, 61455, 61457, 61459, 61460, 61461, 61463, 61464, 61466, 61467, 61468, 61472, 61473, 61475, 61476

K1 2-6-0
62005, 62009, 62046, 62047, 62049, 62056, 62057, 62061, 62063, 62065

J27 0-6-0
65874, 65883, 65885, 65887, 65890, 65894

J94 0-6-0ST
68046, 68061

J72 0-6-0T
68677, 68686, 68687, 68736, 69003, 69008, 69016

3MT 2-6-0
77012

WD 2-8-0
90026, 90045, 90424, 90467, 90518, 90578, 90663

153 Steam locomotives
Class 40
D252, D253, D254, D258, D259, D275, D276, D281, D282, D283, D284, D285

Class 03
D2046, D2062, D2063, D2065, D2066, D2075, D2103, D2110, D2111, D2112, D2113, D2151, D2158, D2159, D2160, D2161

Class 04
D2245, D2268, D2269, D2270

Class 08
D3070, D3071, D3235, D3237, D3238, D3239, D3240, D3313, D3314, D3315, D3318, D3319, D3320, D3872, D3874, D3940, D3946

49 Diesel locomotives

TOTAL 202 Locomotives

STEAM: 4MT 7, 2MT 2, 3F 4, A1 7, A2 8, V2 30, B1 24, B16 38, K1 10, J27 6, J94 2, J72 7, 3MT 1, WD 7

DIESEL: Class 40 12, Class 03 16, Class 04 4, Class 08 17

A TRAIN-SPOTTER'S PARADISE
1950s and 1960s

by Jeff Hodgson

DURING MY FORMATIVE YEARS, I lived on Firth Avenue in Cudworth. My parents' house conveniently, through the gaps between the opposite houses and an area of spare land, gave views of the lines approaching and leaving Cudworth Station and importantly the signals which controlled trains approaching and leaving the station. As soon as the double signals (pegs as we called them) came on, I knew an express was due, and I would make sure I could spot the engine and hopefully cop it. In 1955, I had saved up 2s 6d to purchase my first loco spotter's book. I went to Mellor's Newsagents in Cudworth to buy it. On arriving back home with the book, which had a blue frontage, I soon realised when I showed it to my father, the lists of engines related to engines of the former LNER eg A4s, A3s, A2s, A1s, V2s, B1s, etc, not the engines of the former LMS, seen regularly through

Cudworth Station in 1953.

Black 5 4-6-0 44971 at Cudworth, 30 September 1967, with the 07.06 Sheffield – Leeds train. (P. Hogarth)

Cudworth, so straight away back to the newsagents shop to change it for the locospotter's book containing the numbers and names of the former LMS region eg Black Fives, Patriots, Jubilees, Royal Scots, and of course the BR Standards which at that time were still being built although these were also detailed in the blue LNER book. The locospotter's book for the former LMS had a red frontage. Cudworth was situated on the main line between Leeds and Sheffield and consisted of a six-platform station, five platforms serving the former Midland Railway and one platform serving the former Hull and Barnsley Railway. The passenger service from Hull to Cudworth had finished back in 1932, the station buildings now being used as a traffic control centre.

Cudworth station was an extremely busy station, a train-spotters paradise with a procession of expresses, eg The Thames–Clyde, The Devonian, The Waverley, along with the Leeds–Sheffield stoppers, the specials, the express freights eg The Condor, and the seemingly endless procession of freight approaching and leaving Carlton and Cudworth marshalling yard. There was never a dull moment. Therefore my early trainspotting days were spent predominantly on the station, where the stationmaster would allow my friends and I provided we behaved ourselves to stay and I was on many

RCTS special at Cudworth, class D16 62571, 12 May 1957.

occasions given the honour of being allowed to light the gas lamps on the station along with the lamps down Station Lane. I remember vividly BR Standard Tank Engine 2-6-2T 84009 allocated to Royston shed being used on the Barnsley–Cudworth–Barnsley pull-and-push service. The expresses were in the main hauled by Jubilees, Royal Scots, and occasionally by Britannias predominantly based at Leeds Holbeck shed and to a lesser extent Jubilees on the south-western expresses from Bristol Barrow Road shed [82B]. Therefore it was not long before I had copped the Leeds Holbeck engines, eg Jubilees 45562 *Alberta*, 45564 *New South Wales*, 45566 *Queensland*, 45569 *Tasmania*, 45568 *Western Australia*, 45589 *Gwalior*, 45639 *Raleigh*, 45659 *Drake*, 45694 *Bellerophon*, 45739 *Ulster*, Royal Scots 46103 *Royal Scots Fusilier*, 46112 *Sherwood Forester*, 46113 *Cameronian*, 46145 *The Duke of Wellington's Regiment (West Riding)* and Bristol Barrow Road Jubilees 45690 *Leander* and 45699 *Galatea* (both engines now preserved).

SLS tour at Cudworth, class D20 62360 and class 2P 40726, 20 August 1952.

SLS tour at Cudworth, class 2P 40726, 20 August 1952.

Jubilee 4-6-0 45573 *Newfoundland* standing with a passenger train at platform 1, still wih LMS on the tender but with a BR number, 1948/1951. (A. Ripley)

Near to the station was a field where we would play football. As soon as the signals went on we would stop to note the express passing by. Over a three-day period Patriot 45501 *St Dunstan's* was seen each day. Further Patriots spotted during the football games were 45520 *Llandudno*, 45521 *Rhyl* and 45522 *Prestatyn*, and while bird nesting, an activity wildly frowned upon today and rightly so but a pastime undertaken by most boys of my generation, Royal Scot 46108 *Seaforth Highlander* and Jubilee 45593 *Kolhapur* (now preserved) were seen. During the spring of 1961 as daylight lengthened two of my friends, Graham Day and Arthur Potts, and myself would be on the station to see which engine would be hauling the 7.10 pm. On one occasion as we looked towards Carlton, to our amazement in came the train hauled by Britannia 70054 *Dornoch Firth*. The fireman got down from the engine in the station to uncouple the coaches. I asked the driver if we could come up onto the footplate, please. The driver said Yes and without any hesitation

Britannia Pacific 70054 *Dornoch Firth* **leaves Leeds City in 1960. In 1961 I saw this engine in Cudworth station and even got a ride on the footplate.**
© Jim Carter/Rail Photoprints

we mounted the steps onto the footplate. I was first on and the driver told me to sit on the fireman's seat with my friends standing behind – I was in heaven. Suddenly the driver said, Would you like a ride? Yes please was our reply, and paradise became the next emotion. With the fireman back on the footplate, with a quick blow on the whistle, which was the same sound as a Gresley A4 whistle, the engine pulled off gently, down past Cudworth Station box south, across the points onto the main line. After the points change we proceeded through the station tender first, passed Cudworth Station North box, over Cudworth Bridges, up the junction where the pull-and-push made its way to Barnsley, again a points change, a blow on the whistle, back on the main line over Cudworth bridges again where I waved to people walking on the pavement of the A628 Barnsley–Pontefract road, and back into the station behind the coaches the engine had brought in. The fireman coupled the coaches, the engine shunted them across the main line to couple them up with four more coaches and parked in an adjoining siding. The engine came back into the station where we got off onto the platform, thanking the driver and fireman for the experience of a lifetime. The engine then headed light engine, taking the Chapeltown loop line towards Ardsley Tunnel.

I remember the following engines going through Cudworth straying away from their home ground: B1 61002 *Impala*, and V2 60847 *St Peter's School, York*, AD627. Before leaving my memories of trainspotting on Cudworth station, it is hard to imagine when one walks on the site of the former station today with only the water tower building remaining of this once major station and its surrounds. The line through Cudworth was the first to reach the Barnsley area, opening in 1840 by the North Midland Railway engineered by George Stephenson who avoided gradients wherever possible, therefore Barnsley and Sheffield were bypassed. The station was originally named Barnsley until 1854 when it was renamed Cudworth, as a railway had reached the town of Barnsley in 1850. During our time on the station, to enhance our pocket money we would offer to carry the luggage of passengers alighting from any stopping trains to their nearby destinations, the rewards of which were varied to say the least.

My first venture from Cudworth was to travel by train to nearby Royston for the princely sum of 3d return. The extensive yards at Carlton and Cudworth along with allocation of engines shedded at Royston, although of a freight nature, allowed us to further fill the numbers copped of the 2Fs, 4Fs, 8Fs and WD Austerities, the bonus being also that one could still see all the express passenger and freights which passed through Cudworth further down the line. The next visit further afield, coming twelve months

An un-rebuilt Patriot class 45505 *The Royal Army Ordnance Corps* **at Leeds City station, 29 August 1961.** M. Parker

later, was to Normanton where along with the trains going through Cudworth you got the Leeds–Liverpool traffic. Normanton Station like Cudworth was a grandiose series of buildings, used in earlier times as train changes took place for onward journeys to other parts of the UK, boasting restaurant facilities, a series of platforms, extensive sidings, and a railway shed. Today the area is a shadow of its former self with virtually an island platform only, the sidings and shed long gone. I got around the shed on occasion; the allocation of engines, like Royston, were freight types to deal with predominantly coal traffic.

Spreading further afield, the next journey from Cudworth by train was to the busy centre of Leeds. Virtually every Saturday from 1959 to 1960 was spent on Leeds City Station. The train fare was 1s 6d return. With time

A4 Pacific 60021 *Wild Swan* seen at Doncaster on my first visit. © Rail Photoprints Collection

spent on the station and unofficial visits to Holbeck Shed, my portfolio of engines seen increased considerably, mainly former LMS and BR Standards but also the giants of the former LNER. The first Britannia I saw at Leeds was 70044 *Earl Haig*, followed by 70031 *Byron*, 70032 *Tennyson*, 70034 *Thomas Hardy*, 70035 *Rudyard Kipling*, and 70053 *Moray Firth*, *Earl Haig* and *Moray Firth* being Holbeck engines. My first views of engines of the former LNER had taken place during the journey from Cudworth to Malton, where I and other friends spent a week staying at a youth hostel, arranged through school. We left Cudworth by train to Leeds, onwards to York, changing at York, taking the Scarborough line and getting off at Malton. During the outward and return journeys at York I remember seeing A1s 60135 *Madge Wildfire*, 60142 *Edward Fletcher*, V2 60800 *Green Arrow* and on the journey from York to Leeds Jubilee 45698 *Mars* and at

Leeds City A2 60517 *Ocean Swell*. The first A3 I saw was 60067 *Ladas* at South Kirby on the Leeds–Doncaster line.

Then came the first visit to Doncaster, the Holy Grail to us. It was during the spring of 1960, with three friends, Graham Day, Johnny Corns and Roy Duerden, we caught the 7.05 am bus from Manor Road in Cudworth to Hemsworth Station which was on the Leeds–Doncaster line, catching the 8.23 am train to Doncaster, the train being pulled by a V2 engine. On arrival at Doncaster we made our way across the platforms via the underpass to see the standby engine, which on this day was A1 60130 *Kestrel*. Very soon we heard the chime of an A4 whistle, everyone shouting 'Streak'. A4 60021 *Wild Swan* came in with the Yorkshire Pullman, the engine and coaches a magnificent sight. Shortly after *Wild Swan* and her train left, A4 60006 *Sir Ralph Wedgwood* arrived heading north. After about an hour we left the station and went down to the shed, which amazingly on this occasion we had the freedom to go round; usually doing unofficial visits we were chased out. From the shed we went down to the Plant, scaling the walls and gates to see what engines were on view outside and inside the paint shops. From the plant we made our way to St James's Bridge playing on the tanks awaiting scrapping across from the Doncaster–Sheffield–Barnsley line. As the day drew to a close, it was back to the station to catch the 7.35 pm train getting off at Hemsworth, and then by bus back to Cudworth. To recall all the engines seen on that day, unfortunately the passage of time has dimmed the memory, which makes it difficult to recall all the engines I saw on that day, but I do remember the number of A4s we saw, fourteen in total, but not the 60022 *Mallard*, it had been seen on a visit to Leeds.

This first visit whetted our appetite for many more visits to Doncaster, involving many unofficial visits to the shed and plant, along with time spent on the station, the cattle dock and St James's Bridge. The engines I do remember seeing at various times were A3s 60038 *Firdaussi*, 60039 *Sandwich*, 60045 *Lemberg*, 60049 *Galtee More*, 60052 *Prince Palatine*, 60055 *Woolwinder*, 60074 *Harvester*, 60106 *Flying Fox*, 60109 *Hermit*, 60112 *St Simon*, on the plant stream 60035 *Windsor Lad* and on running in turns 60066 *Merry Hampton* and 60100 *Spearmint*. A1s I recall seeing: 60113 *Great Northern*, 60114 *W.P. Allen*, 60119 *Patrick Stirling*, 60125 *Scottish Union*, 60139 *Sea Eagle*, 60149 *Amadis*, 60156 *Great Central*, 60158 *Aberdonian*. The only A1s I did not see were 60160 *Auld Reekie* and 60161 *North British*. A2s included 60500 *Edward Thompson*, 60512 *Steady Aim*, 60513 *Dante*, 60520 *Owen Tudor*, 60525 *A.H. Peppercorn*, 60528 *Tudor Minstrel*, 60532 *Blue Peter*, and 60539 *Bronzino*. V2s: 60835 *The Green Howard, Alexandra, Princess of Wale's Own Yorkshire Regiment*, 60872

The sad sight of Gresley's first A4. BR No.60014 *Silver Link* on the scrap line at Doncaster Works in 1962. It was not bought for preservation and was finally scrapped in 1963. (P. Buck)

King's Own Yorkshire Light Infantry. B1s 61000 *Springbok*, 61001 *Eland*, 61010 *Wildebeeste*, 61013 *Topi*, 61016 *Inyala*, 61030 *Nyala*, 61040 *Roedeer*.

When making unofficial visits to the plant works, the sight of A3 60102 *Sir Frederick Banbury* being cannibalized for parts for other A3s was sad. The A2 rebuilds of the P2s on the scrapline 60501 *Cock o' the North*, (I saw her nameplates, which were exceptionally long and heavy), 60502 *Earl Marischal*, 60505 *Thane of Fife* and 60506 *Wolf of Badenoch*. Ironically, I never saw probably the most famous locomotive of them all, A3 60103 *Flying Scotsman*, until much later times as 4472 in LNER green livery.

In 1963 I started work at the nearby Redfearns Glass Works at Monk Bretton along with meeting my wife-to-be Joan and my trainspotting days came to a close. However, that interest in railways and in particular steam was soon rekindled and over the last forty years I have regularly visited the preservation centres and photograph the steam specials whenever possible.

A Train-Spotter's Paradise 109

A2 60500 *Edward Thompson* undergoing an overhaul in Doncaster Works, 1959-60. (P. Buck)

STAIRFOOT, BARNSLEY TO DONCASTER, THE CENTRES, THE SPECIALS AND BARRY
1950s and 1960s

by Peter Hadfield

SPENDING THE DAY on Stairfoot station (official name Stairfoot for Ardsley), I was treated to an endless procession of freight engines, in the main transporting coal from the collieries, to the many sidings in the area, of which Stairfoot had a significant number, but primarily to the main marshalling yards at Carlton, Cudworth and Wath. The types of engines seen were Barnsley and Mexborough shed's O1s, O4s, J11s, and WD austerities, along with Royston shed's 4Fs, 8Fs, and WD austerities. I would dream of seeing the Pacifics of the former LNER, A4s, A3s, A2s, and A1s,

RCTS tour at Stairfoot Station in September 1958. The lead engine is B1 61165 with D11 Director 62660 *Butler Henderson* (preserved) behind.

Mexborough B1 61165 leaves Stairfoot with the Barnsley – Doncaster train in the 1950s. Yorkshire Tar Distillers' works can be seen in the background. (P. Hadfield)

along with the V2s, of which at that time I had only seen photographs in my Ian Allan locospotter's book. Passenger traffic through Stairfoot was at a minimum, apart from the excursion traffic to the coast and Belle Vue Zoo in the summer months, along with the enthusiast specials eg The Pennine Pullman and RCTS Tours. The main passenger service was the Penistone–Barnsley–Doncaster trains which consisted of two trains stopping at Stairfoot at approximately 8 am and 10 am with a return service from Doncaster at 6 pm.

The Barnsley–Sheffield Victoria service, via Dovecliffe and Birdwell, had terminated on 7 December 1953, before my time spent on the station. With regard to the Doncaster service, the most glamorous engines I saw were Mexborough and Doncaster shed's Thompson B1s 61165, 61166, 61167, and 61250 *A. Harold Bibby*. On the occasions when the train was working

An unidentified B1 named engine at Stairfoot station awaiting signals before heading to Barnsley with the Doncaster train in the 1950s. (P. Hadfield)

from Cleethorpes an Immingham shed engine was used, the most notable being B1 61379 *Mayflower*. A fish train came through on an evening from the east coast again usually pulled by an Immingham and Doncaster shed's B1. I know that Barnsley shed's J11s and C13 and C14 tank engines, along

Stairfoot signal box 1979. (P. Hadfield)

The site of the former Stairfoot station today, which is now part of the Trans-Pennine Trail. (P. Hadfield)

with occasionally Sheffield Darnall shed's D11 Directors, were used but I cannot recollect seeing them. The nearest railway centre to see the former LNER Pacifics was Doncaster and every time the Doncaster train pulled into Stairfoot station before its closure on 15 September 1957 (after which the train passed straight through), I along with any other of my trainspotting friends, eg John Lunn, Michael Watkin and Ian Caldwell, would look on enviously, dreaming of the day when we would be on the train to Doncaster.

I would have been only 7 or 8 years old at the time and although my parents would allow me to train-spot locally, Doncaster was a bridge too far and understandably so. It is fair to say the 1950s and 1960s was a different era, when youngsters of my generation were allowed by our parents to train-spot, play cricket, football, go to the local woods, climb trees, and during school holidays and weekends be gone most of the day. It was an era of innocence and trust, and our parents would not be worrying about us. Oh how times have sadly changed in our world of today. It is unthinkable that a group of children ranging from the ages of 7 to 12 or 13 would be allowed to undertake the activities we did unsupervised. I was brought up in Kendray, and many of my family both on my mother's and father's side lived in Monk Bretton. I was fortunate to see the many classes of former LMS engines near my home on the Barnsley–Sheffield line, and the Cudworth to Monkspring Junction line which joined the Barnsley–Sheffield line near Swaithe. The Cudworth to Monkspring Junction line was known as the Chapeltown loop line, an alternative route to Sheffield, and when at my relatives in Monk Bretton, ie my Aunty Frances and Uncle Tom's, I would visit Cudworth, Carlton and Cudworth marshalling yards and Royston shed.

I attended Hunningley Lane infant and junior schools which gave views of the Barnsley–Sheffield–Barnsley pull-and-push service worked predominantly by Royston shed's Ivatt tank engines. On the loop line the most prestigious train running Mondays to Saturdays was the up Thames–Clyde express Glasgow St Enoch to London St Pancras which passed over Field Lane bridge at about 3:20 pm. Somehow we called it the three o'clocker, and we knew it was coming when we could see the smoke and steam as it entered and left Ardsley tunnel. At the Junior school if your classroom faced the line the lesson would stop for us to view the train and if you were lucky, which I was on many occasions, allowed outside to get the engine number. The other main booked passenger train of the day was the London St Pancras–Bradford express which again came over Field Lane bridge on the Loop line at 6 pm. Occasionally on the Barnsley–Sheffield line, which is a very busy line today, freights, excursions and diverted trains could be seen, the most memorable being a daily oil train pulled by J11s or B1s, always double-headed. On the loop line around 1:30 pm an express freight heading in the direction of Cudworth would pass, usually pulled by a BR 9F 2-10-0, and at about 7:15 pm again heading in the direction of Cudworth a light engine which could be a Jubilee, a Royal Scot, a Britannia, or a 9F. The most memorable I saw was Britannia 70053 *Moray Firth*. Therefore with the exception of the former LMS Coronation and Princess classes, I saw on a regular basis a number of all the members of the former LMS classes and the BR Standards. Leeds Holbeck Shed 55A had a large allocation of Jubilees, five Royal Scots and three Britannias of which any members could be seen on the Field Lane line or through Cudworth, which at this time was on the Midland main line between Leeds and Sheffield. As the memories come back, the engines I remember seeing were Jubilees 45562 *Alberta*, 45564 *New South Wales*, 45566 *Queensland*, 45568 *Western Australia*, 45589 *Gwalior*, 45639 *Raleigh*, 45658 *Keyes*, 45675 *Hardy*, 45694 *Bellerophon* and 45739 *Ulster*, not forgetting 45612 *Jamaica* which along with 45675 were the first two Jubilees I saw at Swaithe Bridge which was further along the line after Monkspring Junction. Royal Scots 46103 *Royal Scots Fusilier*, 46112 *Sherwood Forester*, 46113 *Cameronian*, 46145 *The Duke of Wellington's Regt (West Riding)* and finally Britannias 70044 *Earl Haig* were noted, and as previously mentioned 70053 *Moray Firth*. *Alberta*, *Keyes*, and *Ulster* were often regulars on the Thames–Clyde and London–Bradford expresses and as my friends and I were keen to cop different locos we would boo and sometimes shout 'scrap it'. How we regret those words today.

My first real view of the LNER Pacifics came when my parents and I went on holiday to Scotland in 1959. My father had been a prisoner of war under the Japanese during the Second World War, and despite the brutality handed out to him and his army colleagues, he survived whereas many did not. One of his friends who been with him in the camps and worked alongside him on the infamous death railway was Scottish and lived with his family in Markinch in Fife. I can only remember his first name, which was Jim, and every couple of years, along with his wife, they would visit us, coming on a motorcycle. What a journey that must have been. We were invited to visit them around March/April which was cordially accepted, travelling by train. We left Barnsley Exchange station, which was only a one-platform station with an adjoining steam shed, by diesel multiple unit to Leeds. The former Exchange station is now part of the Transport Interchange. From Leeds we caught the North Briton pulled by York shed's A1 60121 *Silurian*. I was allowed by my parents to see the engine before departure, not having the confidence to ask the driver if I could come up onto the footplate as I stood in awe of this magnificent locomotive, which at this time would

York based A1 Pacific 60121 *Silurian*. This engine pulled us on my Scotland holiday, hauling the North Briton train.
© Alan Turnbull/Rail Photoprints Collection

be around ten years old. Sadly it was to have only a further working life of five/six years before being withdrawn by British Railways such was the haste to banish steam, including locos of new designs, bearing in mind it was considered that a steam locomotive would normally have a working life of about thirty to forty years. The BR Standard classes and in particular the 9Fs did not have a working life in many cases of ten years, which many considered to be criminal. The Modernisation Plan of 1955 was to gradually replace steam with diesel and electric traction, which would have seen modern steam designs operating into the 1970s being replaced by proven, reliable diesel and electric traction. In the case of diesel traction this was certainly not the case, as many types introduced in the late fifties and early sixties were not up to standard which resulted in many failures. The benefit of this was that steam still had a strong presence for a time. The journey to Scotland was awesome, passing York, Darlington, Gateshead, where I saw my first A4 60009 *Union of South Africa*, and Newcastle before reaching Edinburgh Waverley station. A change of train took us over the magnificent Forth Bridge, leaving the train at Kirkcaldy, where A2 60535 *Hornets Beauty* was in the station, then by bus to Markinch. After the holiday we travelled back on the Queen of Scots Pullman, which my father had to pay extra for much to his annoyance. The engine to take us back to Leeds was again York's A1 60121 *Silurian*. On the journey to Scotland, I was given a telling-off from my mother for not taking an interest in the history of the castles

Court House Junction, Barnsley, in the 1950s. P. Hadfield

seen on the way, being told to me by a lady sitting near us. My only thoughts were concentrating on the engines I saw.

   The Scotland holiday further reinforced my desire to gain permission to go to Doncaster. That day arose pretty quickly, as many of my friends in the streets where we lived were planning a visit to Doncaster, trainspotting for the day. As some of my friends were older than me I was allowed to go along with other friends of my age. As Stairfoot station had closed by now, we had to go by bus from Kendray to catch the train from Barnsley

Ivatt class 2-6-0 46494 enters Barnsley Court House station with a passenger train in the 1950s. P. Hadfield

Class J11 0-6-0 64387 arrives at Court House station from Penistone, 1950s.
P. Hadfield

B1 4-6-0 61166 in Barnsley Court House station in the 1950s. P. Hadfield

Ivatt class 2, 2-6-2T 41251 enters Barnsley Exchange with the Leeds – Barnsley – Leeds service prior to 1958-59, when DMUs took over.

Court House station, which we did not know at the time would only be open for through trains for another year. Barnsley Court House station was very aesthetically pleasing and well built, and far more appealing than the Exchange station, and was in fact the reason the Midland Railway built the station opening in 1870 because of the poor image the Exchange station

Pennine Pullman on the through road in Barnsley Exchange on 12 May 1956. The lead engine is D11 Director 62664 *Princess Mary*.

A 1966 view of Exchange station. The shed has been demolished, although some sidings have been retained. B1 4-6-0 61237 of Wakefield shed is the motive power on this Wakefield – Barnsley service standing at the new platform erected upon closure of Court House station in April 1960. P. Hogarth

Barnsley shed's 04 63913 in the siding adjacent to Needham & Brown's Foundry in the 1950s.

Rear of Pennine Pullman train going over Jumble Lane Crossing heading to Stairfoot, 12 May 1956.

Jubilee 45581 *Bihar & Orissa* passes through Summer Lane station in August 1965 with the Saturdays only Poole – Bradford service.

Jubilee 45562 *Alberta* passes Summer Lane signal box with the Poole – Bradford train on a summer Saturday in 1965/66.

portrayed. Apart from the Leeds–Barnsley service operating from Exchange station, all other passenger services operated from Court House station. The train started its journey from Penistone, calling at Silkstone, Dodworth, and Summer Lane, to pick up passengers before arrival at Barnsley Court House station. The anticipation and excitement of the day started on the bus journey listening to the older boys who had been to Doncaster many times recalling the engines they had seen and hoping I would spot the same engines, see the non-stop Elizabethan, and the Flying Scotsman trains and which engines would be pulling them. The Yorkshire Pullman, the Tees-Tyne Pullman, added to the day's anticipation, along with what the standby engine would be, as well as the many other expresses and freights and the locos on shed and in the works.

The Court House station building (still standing today and used as a public house) was the main entrance to the station. You collected your ticket from the ticket office situated on the ground floor, then up a flight

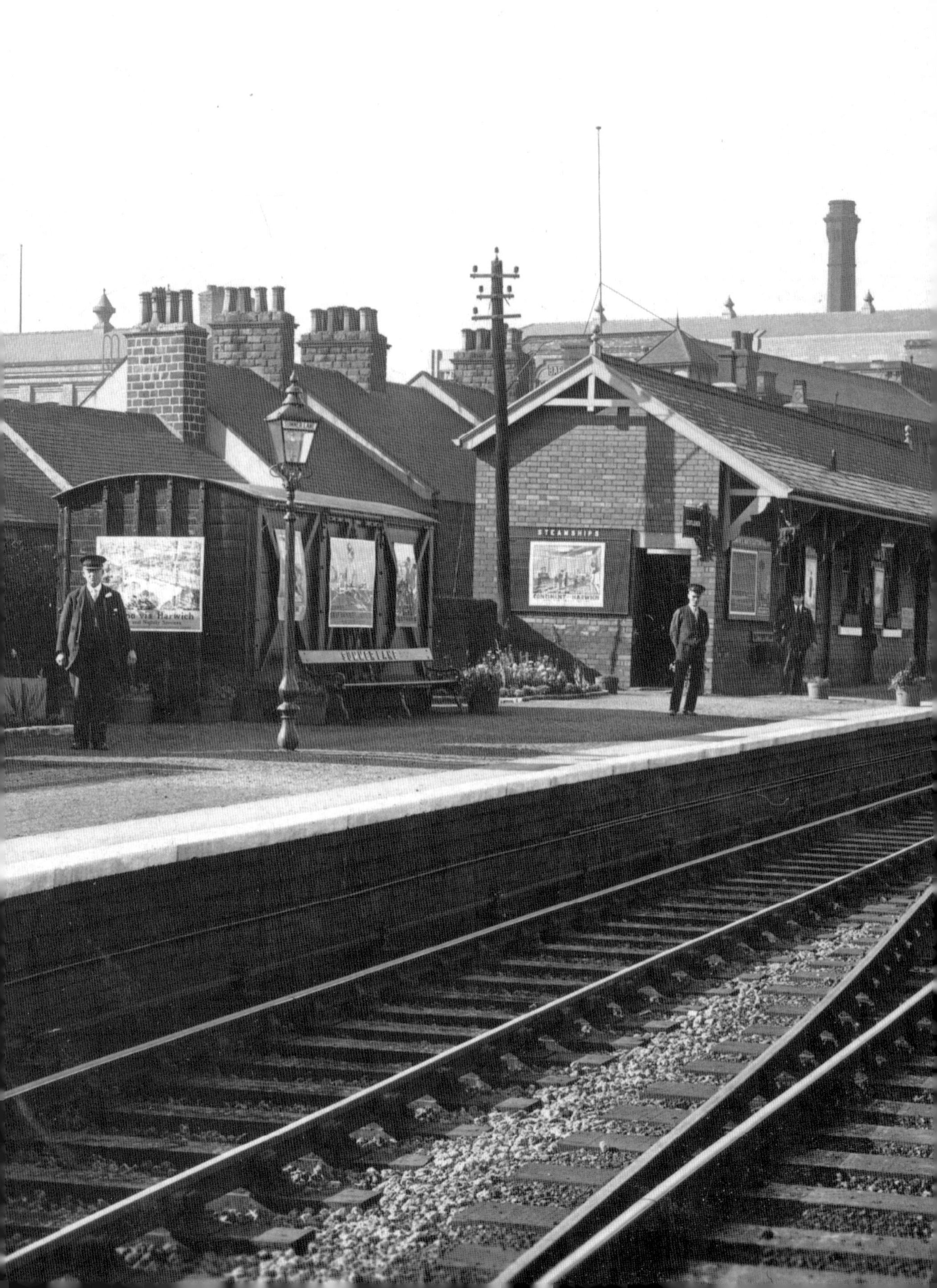
STEAMSHIPS

Summer Lane station photographed in 1929. The station won awards for its neat and tidy appearance. The station closed 29 June 1959 after termination of the Penistone–Barnsley–Doncaster service. The station was still used for excursion traffic.

Jubilee 4-6-0 45581 *Bihar & Orissa* approaches Summer Lane with the Bradford – Poole train during the summer of 1965/66. The CWS buildings are on the left.

Jubilee 4-6-0 45643 *Rodney* at Summer Lane heading to Barnsley with the same train on another summer Saturday, 19 May 1966.

The Penistone–Barnsley–Doncaster train photographed from Oakwell Lane being hauled by a J11, probably from Barnsley shed, during June 1955. P.J. Lynch

of stairs to reach platform level, the station being above ground level. The engine pulling our train was B1 61266, departing at 9:54 am and leaving the station by means of a brick viaduct running above but adjacent to the bus station then crossing the Exchange line via a steel lattice bridge near to the former Ceag and Needham and Brown's factories, before running alongside the Exchange line at Oakwell Lane. At Barnsley West we joined the line to

Summer Lane signal box.

A Class J39 locomotive passes Mitchell Main with a passenger train in the 1950s heading towards Wombwell. P. Hadfield

Stairfoot, whereas the line to Cudworth carried straight on following the route around Barnsley Main Colliery Spoil Heaps. The line to Sheffield crossed the Stairfoot line by means of a steel girder bridge, later to be known as Quarry Junction after engineering work in 1960 to connect the Stairfoot and Sheffield lines to enable direct running into Exchange station and the closure of Court House station. We then passed Barnsley Main Colliery and through Stairfoot station which brought back many memories of the times I had been on the station when it was open and the train stopped to pick up passengers. We proceeded on towards Wombwell, passing Yorkshire Tar Distillers and Stairfoot Brickworks at Aldam Junction, then joined the electrified line part of the Wath–Penistone–Sheffield–Manchester Woodhead route. Around the sidings of Mitchell Main and Darfield Main collieries, I remember a shunter named *William Pepper* working on the line from Elsecar and Cortonwood collieries joining the main line. Later in life I would work for the Hargreaves Group of Companies, where I was informed that the William Pepper company, who were actively in the screening of coal, were part of the Group and hence the engine carried the name. The next stop was Wombwell Central station on Station Lane before proceeding towards Wath. At Elsecar Junction, Wath marshalling yard was passed through, a huge collection of sidings working on a hump principle, the yard having opened in 1907. Diesel shunters and electric traction in the

Stairfoot, Barnsley to Doncaster, the Centres, the Specials and Barry 127

Wombwell Central station looking towards Wath. (C. Sharp)

The site of Wombwell Central station in 1981. The tracks and overhead wires have since been removed and it now forms part of the Trans-Pennine Trail.
P. Hadfield

Wath yard and shed, 5 October 1980. (P. Hadfield)

Class 20 diesels at Wath yard, 6 July 1981. P. Hadfield

Two class 20s and a Brush Type 2 class 31 at Wath shed, 6 July 1981. P. Hadfield

Peak class 45 at Wath shed. (P. Hadfield)

The site of Wath Central station looking towards Manvers, October 1980.
(P. Hadfield)

form of the EM1s were the mainstay of the motive power. In the main, coal trains were prepared for onward transportation to the power stations. Wath had its own shed although steam from Barnsley and Mexborough sheds could still be seen. Wath Central station was our next stop, and along with Wombwell Central no traces can be seen today. On leaving Wath Central station we entered the industrial heart of the Wath area, around Wath Staithes crossing. The huge Manvers Coking Plant, Manvers Colliery, the

The last Penistone – Doncaster train at Wath Central, June 1959. The loco is a class C14 4-4-2T No. 67445.

Class 2P 4-4-0 40487 in Mexborough station on a rail tour, 1953.

Mexborough station, October 1980. P. Hadfield

NCB workshops, offices and laboratories, were passed before going under the former Midland Railway bridges at Wath Road Junction where the lines split to Cudworth and York. This location was also a good loco-spotting place as you saw the rail traffic from Sheffield and Rotherham passing through, taking either the Cudworth line to Leeds or the former Swinton and Knottingley line through Bolton-upon-Dearne up to York, with the added bonus of the Barnsley–Wath–Mexborough–Doncaster traffic passing underneath the Wath Road bridges. Our next stop was Mexborough with its large shed visible on the right. The shed was a freight shed with a large contingent of O1s, O4s, J11s and WD Austerities. It had a number of Thompson B1s and was home at one time for the famous Garratt that worked on the steep gradient of the Wentworth Bank of the Wath–Penistone section of the Woodhead Route. The Wath Tinies shunting engines which worked in Wath yard before electrification were also shedded there. On leaving Mexborough we passed the power station, across Denaby Crossing, past Denaby Main and Cadeby collieries, our next stop being Conisborough station, where in one period a relative of the actor Donald Pleasance had been stationmaster. From Conisborough the castle could be seen, and the limestone geology made a pleasing view before finally entering Doncaster station. That day at Doncaster, the variety of locomotives seen! My second A4 60021 *Wild Swan* on the Yorkshire Pullman, a visit to the shed and

A filthy J11 at Conisbrough with a passenger train, 1953.

Conisbrough station, October 1980. P. Hadfield

35028 Merchant Navy *Clan Line* in York, 1979. The tour was the York – Harrogate circular and the author is pictured by the locomotive. P. Hadfield

A4 60009 *Union of South Africa* in Aberdeen station on the Edinburgh – Aberdeen – Edinburgh special run in September 1979. P. Hadfield

Barry scrapyard. Ex-GWR 7927 *Willington Hall* and a 9F 2-10-0, October 1978. P. Hadfield

scaling the walls of the plant works before returning on the train leaving at approximately 5 pm, will forever be etched in my memory. This visit was to be the first of numerous visits, which after the train service was curtailed it was by the No14 bus from Stairfoot Coop, now Worsboro Motor Spares, and finally on my bicycle.

To conclude my chapter I would like to briefly mention the journeys I made following the lifting of the steam ban on the main line in the 1970s: Merchant Navy 35028 *Clan Line* on the York–Harrogate circular, the Welsh Marches behind Stanier Pacific 46229 *Duchess of Hamilton*, the Settle–Carlisle trips at various times behind A4 60009 *Union of South Africa*, West Country Pacific 34092 *City of Wells*, the Midland Compound and Jubilee 5690 *Leander*, Edinburgh to Aberdeen and return behind A4 *Union of South Africa* and Peterborough–York with A3 4472, 60103 *Flying Scotsman*.

The visits to Barry scrapyard are memorable journeys which will stay with me forever.

Finally came visits to the museums and steam centres, eg The National

Barry scrapyard. Ex-Crab LMS 42859, SR Merchant Navy 35027 in the foreground, with an ex-GWR Pannier Tank, August 1979. P. Hadfield

A4 *Bittern* and A2 *Blue Peter* stored at Walton Colliery yard, near Wakefield, December 1975. Both engines were not in the best condition, but have now, thankfully, been restored. P. Hadfield

Rail Museum York, Carnforth, Tinsley, Dinting, Barrow Hill and seeing the steam specials that passed periodically on the York–Sheffield line at Bolton upon Dearne, through Doncaster and the Scarborough Spa express through Wakefield.

All are a reminder of glorious memories of a time gone by.

Carnforth Steam Centre, 'Steamtown', summer 1978. Blacks 5s 45407 and 44932 are shown. P. Hadfield

PENISTONE
1950s

by Aldred Bostwick

MY EARLIEST MEMORIES of my interest in railways started with the journey by Yorkshire Traction bus from Hoylandswaine to Barnsley, stopping at Dodworth level crossing as the National Coal Board shunter was propelling coal wagons from the colliery on the line preparing them, for a British Railways locomotive to take them predominantly to Penistone sidings for onward transportation to the various coal fired power stations. I remember the old wooden signal box being destroyed when a number of coal wagons ran away colliding with the signal box, ultimately demolishing it. The signal box was rebuilt as a brick structure, and survives today. In the early 1950s in the school holidays I would go with my mother and grandmother on the train from Penistone to Huddersfield on market days.

I have always had a keen interest in cricket, both from a playing and

Manchester-bound passenger train at Dunford bridge hauled by EM2 E27006, stripped of its *Pandora* nameplates, 28 February 1968. M. Parker

B1 61247 *Lord Burghley* leaving Penistone with a special in the 1950s. P. Hadfield

non-playing perspective, that interest is still with me today. With my uncle, when Yorkshire were playing at Bramall Lane, we would catch the train from Penistone to Sheffield Victoria being hauled by steam and electric traction, from where we would walk to the cricket ground. In 1956, eight of my friends including me were allowed to travel to Old Trafford, Manchester, to watch England versus Australia. The locomotive hauling us from Penistone to Manchester was an EM2 electric loco and one of the highlights of the journey was going through the new Woodhead Tunnel which was lit up throughout. The tunnel only opening two years earlier in 1954.

My father worked as a lorry and coach driver for Fearns transport based in Dodworth. On summer weekends he would take me with him on trips, the highlight being the trips to Blackpool where the coach park was situated next to Blackpool locomotive shed. At the height of the summer the shed was crowded with locomotives that had brought in excursion trains to the resort from all parts of the country, but mainly from the North, the Midlands and Scotland. The engines were mainly Black Fives, Patriots, Jubilees, Royal Scots and an occasional Coronation class.

My trainspotting was restricted to Penistone back in the early 1950s. A friend and I were allowed to go on our bicycles on our own to the station where we would spend all day. Penistone was a major station and had a cafe serving snacks and hot meals. People from the centre of Penistone

Class D11 Director 62666 *Zeebrugge* and a C13/14 tank approach Penistone in the 1950s.

would come to have lunch and we would be given money by our parents to have steak pie and chips. When we first started trainspotting, the motive power was all steam, and there were regular excursions in summer to Blackpool and Belle Vue Amusement Park in Manchester heading west, and in the easterly direction to Cleethorpes, mainly hauled by Black Fives and Thompson B1s. The Woodhead route through Penistone carried a

Black 5 4-6-0 44947 on the Sunday monthly excursion Doncaster- Blackpool- Doncaster, photographed at West Silkstone Junction, May 1959. The electrified line can be seen on the left (Wath – Penistone).

An eastbound rake of coal empties leaving the Woodhead tunnel and passing through Dunford bridge, 28 February 1968. M. Parker

large amount of goods traffic to and from the marshalling yards at Wath and Rotherwood. My grandfather worked at Penistone Goods depot. The goods traffic in steam days was hauled by class O1s, O4s and WD Austerity locomotives. On the Wath–Penistone section they were helped up the

Aldred Bostwick's grandad (right) working at Penistone.

Penistone – Barnsley – Doncaster train in Penistone station. An immaculately clean C13 tank 4-4-2T 67434 of Barnsley shed is the motive power.

gradient between Wentworth and West Silkstone Junction by the famous Beyer-Garratt locomotive.

Regular trains to Barnsley and Doncaster were hauled by C13 and C14 tanks along with Thompson B1s, the most notable being 61250 *A. Harold Bibby*. One busy train was the David Brown special which was for the employees who worked at the nearby David Brown foundry. This train left at 5 pm with five coaches, destination Barnsley. The regular service to Huddersfield and Bradford was hauled by a Fairburn tank locomotive. When the line was initially electrified in stages from 1952 to 1954 the passenger services from Sheffield to Manchester were hauled from Sheffield Victoria to Penistone by steam, usually by a B1. The engine was detached at

4MT 2-6-4T 42112 arrives at Penistone from Bradford Exchange, April 1950. Aldred Bostwick remembers these engines at the station and travelling to Huddersfield with this motive power pulling the train.

Penistone and electric traction in the form of EM1s or EM2s then took the train to Manchester. The steam engine was stabled at Penistone ready to take a train back to Sheffield. The South Yorkshireman came from Bradford usually hauled by a Thompson B1, and even after the line was electrified in 1954, for a time, steam still headed the train to Sheffield. The Liverpool–Harwich Boat train pre-electrification was hauled regularly by a Gresley A3 Pacific but following electrification EM1s or EM2s took the train to

Climbing up from Thurlstone, EM1 26053, formerly *Perseus*, on a westbound coal train. M. Parker

Penistone station. J11 0-6-0 64442 waits to depart with a passenger train.

Abandoned Woodhead route and abandoned platforms at Penistone after the route was closed on 18 July 1981. P. Hadfield

Woodhead Tunnel entrance, September 1983. (P. Hadfield)

Sheffield Victoria where steam power in the form of an A3, a Sandringham or a Britannia, then took over for the onward journey to Harwich. After electrification of the Wath–Penistone section in 1952, EM1s took over from steam on this section of the line which was used for goods traffic only. They are such vivid memories of a unique time of my life.

Penistone station is now a shadow of its former self. The Woodhead route closed in 1981 and the platforms are long gone along with the track, the route through to Hadfield now being part of the Trans-Pennine Trail. The Woodhead Tunnel is inaccessible at both the Woodhead and Dunford Bridge entrances, being used to carry through electric cables. Thankfully the station buildings on the former Woodhead platform to Sheffield are used as offices along with the former control building, and the station is still open with the Huddersfield platforms for the Sheffield–Barnsley–Huddersfield service and the return service stopping at the station on a regular basis.

The Huddersfield platforms at Penistone after closure of the Woodhead route, 18 July 1981.

BARNSLEY AND BEYOND
1950s

by Michael Watkin

I CANNOT REMEMBER when I began trainspotting, but it must have been as soon as I could walk. My first 'namer' was 61250 *A. Harold Bibby*, a Doncaster B1. The loco was on Barnsley shed and I was so excited that I asked a railwayman if it was a 'namer'. Barnsley was full of ex-LNER and Great Central locomotives allocated to the shed for transporting coal and other freight and accommodating and servicing locomotives from other sheds. I remember the 4-4-2 tank engines 67445, 67439, 67447, just to mention a few. We would go to Penistone and Cudworth behind one of these locos many times until they were replaced by other power such as Ivatt's 2-6-2 tank engines particularly on the Cudworth service from Barnsley. Both sets of my grandparents lived on Sherwood Street and many times I would walk over Jumble Lane level crossing and observe the many locos that were stabled on Barnsley shed and jump for joy if a B1 was to be seen. Many specials passing through Barnsley were hauled by B1s. Many

EM1 locos 26011, 26010 and 26007 enjoying a rest day on Wath depot, 2 January 1962. M. Parker

EM1 26048 *Hector* at Swaithe, 1960. Michael Watkin recalls his trainspotting days at this location. A. Godfrey

times my pals and I went to Cudworth on the Cudworth Flyer from Court House station and when trainspotting sat on the wall by the road that led up to the station. We were forbidden to train-spot on the station platforms.

I would cycle to Wath after school and during the school holidays to see the EM1s and occasionally an EM2 loco along with the numerous steam locomotives in the huge marshalling yard shunting wagons and then leaving for unknown destinations with 16-ton mineral wagons rattling behind. We would train-spot on the Wath–Penistone electrified line below Swaithe Bridge to see the electrics and an occasional steam loco pass by. I loved the EM1s especially the named ones, I have the model 26056 *Triton*. The woods on the far side of the line were called 'Black Pad' for some reason or another and we would dare one another to go into the woods because tramps would sometimes camp there.

EM1 76051 banks a loaded coal train away from Wombwell Main. Swaithe viaduct can be seen in the background. © Rail Photoprints Collection/John Chalcraft

On a trainspotting trip to Sheffield Midland station with my brothers Alan and Keith and friends one day, we had the choice either to go to Millhouses shed or go to Sheffield Victoria station to see the Boat train. We chose Victoria Station and Britannia 70001 *Lord Hurcomb* arrived with the Boat train. I remember quite well copping Patriot class 45519 *Lady Godiva* on a passenger service back at Midland station.

How could I ever forget Field Lane Bridge near Hunningley Lane Primary School, where my pals Peter Hadfield, John Lunn and myself attended the school. The Thames–Clyde express passed only a short distance from the school and many times our teacher would allow us to go out and stand on the school yard wall and get the engine number. The engine was nearly always a Jubilee class locomotive shedded at Leeds Holbeck shed. We would watch The Thames–Clyde express come out of Ardsley Tunnel and when we could see if it was a Black Five or a Jubilee engine that regularly hauled the train, for example 45562 *Alberta* which seemed to be permanently attached to the train, we would shout 'scrap it', so unfairly and how we regret that

Heading towards Stairfoot, 8F 48055 rounds the curve with a coal train. The disused Ardsley Tunnel can be seen in the distance. The photograph was taken in 1965. Les Nixon

45562 *Alberta* at Bradford Exchange 1967. This was an engine we saw regularly around Barnsley, so much so that we would shout 'scrap it'. An unfortunate term looking back as it was eventually scrapped which is a pity.
© Norman Preedy/Rail Photoprints

Royal Scot 46102 *Black Watch* phtographed at the Carlisle Citadel in 1958. I saw this engine at Field Lane on its way to Sheffield.
© Rail Photoprints Collection

comment – to see *Alberta* running today would be fantastic. All the Holbeck Jubilees did appear over time, although one day I recall not going to see The Thames–Clyde express, I must have been ill, and one of my school friends told me that Jubilee 45689 *Ajax* complete with red nameplates was in charge of the express. Around 7 pm each weekday a 9F would come past Field Lane heading towards Ardsley Tunnel and Cudworth with a fitted freight, and heading in the opposite direction towards Sheffield, a single light engine would pass.

I will never forget, Royal Scot 46102 *Black Watch* was the engine one evening and seeing the engine which was based in Scotland was an unreal cop. I have read in many publications that this engine did venture into our area. I have the Bachmann model, which captures the memory of that particular evening.

Trainspotting at Field Lane also got me in trouble. Hardly the crime of the century but a group of us were prosecuted for trespassing on the railway. I went to court and being about 7 or 8 years old was fined 10 shillings (50p), banned from trainspotting by my father and had my train books confiscated. I had my Hornby Dublo locos 46232 *Duchess of Montrose*, 69567 and 80064 to play with while I was serving my punishment. I went off again doing the thing I loved most, trainspotting, when I was allowed out again.

I also remember riding to Fitzwilliam station one Sunday with one of my school friends, sadly I cannot recall who, and we copped A4 60022 *Mallard*.

The A4 was heading in the Doncaster direction from Leeds. This was the only time I ever went to Fitzwilliam and of course nobody would believe us, about copping *Mallard,* especially my two brothers.

Doncaster was a fantastic place to train-spot. We went there many times and we used to get off the bus before it arrived at the station. It was quicker to walk than stay on the bus. Even Doncaster road traffic at this time was bumper to bumper. I saw my first A1 60125 *Scottish Union* running light engine back to Doncaster shed. Sitting on the wall with everyone else by the cattle dock watching the expresses hauled by the A4s, A3s, A2s, A1s and V2s was fantastic along with the express freights. On one trainspotting trip a rumbling sound was heard in the far distance and we more or less realised that the prototype Blue Deltic was coming. The Deltic roared through on an express heading north. A sight never to be forgotten. I also have the model in my collection. The Plant steam and Shed steam were also a highlight. Filthy locos coming in for repair or overhaul and shiny gleaming engines fresh from the works going on to Doncaster Shed. We used to send my eldest brother Alan for fish and chips at lunchtime, and always something out of the ordinary would appear and he would miss out on copping it. My two brothers Alan and Keith did not last long into trainspotting; they made a few trips only, it was me who was the hobbyist. I remember on a trip to Leeds, Alan, the eldest, was

Doncaster's A1 60125 *Scottish Union* was the first A1 I saw at Doncaster.

Jubilee 45730 *Ocean* which I saw through the carriage window on the train back from Leeds to Barnsley. A picture of this engine was in my ABC combined volumes and I always hoped I would see it. © Colin Whitfield/Rail Photoprints

in charge of the camera and when we had the film developed all we had to show was the railway lines. He had the camera pointed too low.

Leeds was also a destination not to be missed. We went round Holbeck shed a few times and actually walked round unchallenged. Here were the three Holbeck Britannia class locos which were duly copped, 70044 *Earl Haig*, 70053 *Moray Firth* and my favourite 70054 *Dornoch Firth*. Once again I have The Thames–Clyde Express model pack with *Dornoch Firth* being the loco. The only Clan I remember seeing at Leeds was 72006 *Clan Mackenzie*. All the Jubilees, Black Fives and the newer BR Standards would be on shed. Trainspotting on Leeds City station, we would see the Thames–Clyde express arrive and many times I saw a Royal Scot class loco was in charge coming off the Settle and Carlisle line. My favourite was 46103 *Royal Scots Fusilier* being a 55A Leeds Holbeck engine. One day when we were there, when the Scot came to a standstill one of the older boys held a large piece of paper and was

An early photograph of Stairfoot station. We would sit on the platform and watch locos go past mainly hauling coal wagons.

rubbing it over the nameplate to make an imprint.

Only in later years have I found out where many of the railway lines used to go by having so many railway books, magazines and films. Being so young I never knew that the through platforms at Leeds City station went past Neville Hill shed and subsequently in the York direction and often wondered where the viaduct above Holbeck shed went. I believe it carried the Newcastle–Liverpool expresses and vice versa. I do recall a Baby Scot come in on the through platforms and leave over the viaduct but could not remember the number.

In one of my ABC combined volumes was a picture of Jubilee 45730 *Ocean* and coming home by train from Leeds back to Barnsley we saw a Jubilee through the carriage window. I said, 'I hope it is *Ocean*,' and unbelievably it was 45730 *Ocean*. I cherished my combined volumes and my favourite was the Summer 1960 edition with an A3 and a Type 4 diesel, later class 40, on the cover. The book was lost many years ago, but I managed to pick up a copy online. I still possess The Observers Book of British Locomotives from around 1960.

My friends and I would sit on Stairfoot station watching the locos go past mainly hauling coal wagons from the many collieries around Barnsley. I remember when Barnsley Court House station closed and a gradient was built dropping down from the Sheffield line at Quarry Junction so trains could run direct into Barnsley Exchange station. Going to my grandparents' houses by bus we could see the work being carried out into the evenings under masses of lights.

In 1960 my father decided to take us to live in Australia, so in January

The *Flying Scotsman* preparing to depart Keswick railway station in Adelaide, South Australia, with a northbound special, August 1989. M. Watkin

The *Flying Scotsman* pausing at Two Wells, north of Adelaide, with admirers looking on. M. Watkin

1961 my family emigrated thus leaving my beloved locomotives behind. In pouring rain and in the middle of the night, one of my uncles drove us to Sheffield to catch the train to London. I was about 11 years old and leaving everybody behind was very upsetting, my friends and relatives gone. Crying and saying that final goodbye when our train came in hauled by a Royal Scot, I was too upset to get the name and number. The next day – I think the train was hauled by an Ivatt Mogul 2-6-0 – we arrived at Tilbury Docks and boarded the SS *Orontes* for our trip to Australia, my best friends John Lunn and Peter Hadfield and relations left behind.

Australia held its bicentennial in 1988 and *Flying Scotsman* came to Australia for the event but stayed for over a year. I would never have dreamed 27 years after leaving England I would see an A3 again. Living in Adelaide at the time I was lucky to see the loco a few times while it was there and running excursions.

The *Flying Scotsman* and South Australian broad gauge 4-6-2 Pacific number 621 *Duke of Edinburgh* run parallel through North Adelaide with many of the specials, when the *Flying Scotsman* was in South Australia, August 1989. M. Watkin

THE SMOKE, THE SMELL, THE STEAM
1948 – 1955

by Brian Mathers

I WAS BORN in Cundy Cross, a suburb of Barnsley, my bedroom window giving iconic views of the intense railway network surrounding the area along with the majestic ruins of Monk Bretton Priory and the meandering River Dearne. The panorama included Stairfoot station, the Chapeltown Loop line with its brick viaduct bridging Stairfoot and the line disappearing into Ardsley Tunnel, the former Hull and Barnsley railway skirting along the boundary of Lundwood, finally meeting its terminus, joining the Barnsley–Doncaster line at Stairfoot Junction, the Barnsley Coal Railway with its high embankment of the Stairfoot Curve, and finally the single mineral line from Stairfoot to Houghton and Grimethorpe collieries,

The Pennine Pullman heads through Stairfoot station on 12 May 1956 with D11 Directors 62664 *Princess Mary* **and 62662** *Prince of Wales* **pulling the train.**

A. Harold Bibby **at Doncaster in 1961.** © Paul Claxton/Rail Photoprints

bridging the A633 road on Grange Lane. The scene was set to enjoy the local railway network before venturing further afield.

Being born in the early 1940s, I can vividly remember the nationalisation of the railways in 1948, with the big four companies, the LNER, the LMS, the Great Western, and the Southern Railway, being unified into one organisation: British Railways. For the first couple of years the locomotives and the rolling stock retained their former companies' liveries before being transformed after trial liveries into British Railways black, brunswick green and red liveries, dependent on the class and type of locomotives.

Stairfoot was the obvious starting point for trainspotting, although the traffic was mainly of a freight nature. I was treated to Thompson's B1 named engines (eg 61237 *Geoffrey H. Kitson*, 61246 *Lord Balfour of Burleigh*, 61247 *Lord Burghley*, 61248 *Geoffrey Gibbs*, 61250 *A. Harold Bibby*, 61251 *Oliver Bury*, and 61379 *Mayflower*) on the Penistone–Barnsley–Doncaster service, and the fish train from Grimsby, which passed through the station during the evening around 21.00 hours sometimes stopping for a banker to help with the gradient up to Barnsley. The names of the Lords and the Sirs made me dream of their history. The Chapeltown Loop line over Stairfoot gave us the chance to see the Travelling Post Office, The Thames–Clyde express and the London–Bradford express along with the many freights, specials, and light engines.

My pals Johnny Hancock and Arthur Ayrton had the same interest in railways as me, and after Stairfoot we started to venture further afield. Arthur was the same age as me, but Johnny was four years older. He looked after us and my parents had complete trust in him. Cudworth was the next place to build up our collection of locomotive numbers. Cudworth was on the former LMS main line between Leeds and Sheffield and there we were treated to what seemed to be an endless procession of express passenger, local passenger services, and freights. The named passenger trains were the Thames–Clyde, Glasgow St Enoch–London St Pancras, the Devonian, Bradford–Paignton, the Waverley, Edinburgh–London St Pancras, the London–Bradford service and the local Leeds–Sheffield service, as well as the return services of all the aforementioned. Sitting on the wall on Station Road, adjacent to the access road from Cudworth Bridges, we were never more than thirty yards from the trains. Jubilees, Royal Scots, Patriots, and Britannias regularly hauled the trains. My favourites were the Jubilees, for apart from what I considered to be a handsome looking engine, their names further enhanced my education. The names of the former colonies of the British Empire, such as *Australia*,

Jubilee 4-6-0 45662 *Kempenfell* **leaves Cudworth in the early 1950s. The access road to the station from Cudworth bridge is in the foreground, with trainspotters perched on the wall, a memory Brian remembers well.** A. Ripley

A4 Pacific 60033 *Seagull* leaving York station with a northbound service, 1958. This was the first A4 I saw as we were train spotting at Hemsworth on the Leeds–Doncaster line. © Alan H. Bryant/Rail Photoprints

South Africa, Canada and *India*; state names, *Alberta, Nova Scotia, Western Australia, Queensland* and *Tasmania*; British admirals, *Hardy, Nelson, Drake*; great sea battles, *Jutland* and *Trafalgar*; and the warships *Victory, Bellerophon, Hood* and *Renown*, all helped with history and geography.

On summer evenings, on occasions we would go on our bicycles to Hemsworth, which was on the Leeds–Doncaster line. As previously mentioned, in early British Railways days, different liveries were tried along with the former company liveries. On my first visit to Hemsworth, with Johnny and Arthur sitting on the fence adjacent to the road bridge above the railway cutting, at about 18.00 we heard the unforgettable chime whistle of an A4 Pacific (a streak), my first. It stopped with its nose protruding out from the bridge, painted in the beautiful blue livery of the LNER and named *Seagull*. A short while later on the down line nearest to us on a through express, A1 *Great Northern* hauling immaculate teak coloured coaches thundered past. Two magnificent memories.

Our next venture was to what was regarded by many of us as the railway mecca: Doncaster. We caught the 10.00 train from Stairfoot station to Doncaster and on arrival on the platforms, the sound and sight of a streak (A4) – what a memory . There was so many trains my pencil could not write fast enough, tank engines going back and forth, then suddenly an express, which could be hauled by any of the Pacifics, an A4, A3, A2, A1, or a V2. We would be moved off the station, grudgingly, by one of the porters, from where we would make our way down to St James's Bridge, down the ramp which was already full of boys with the same motive as us. We were called anoraks, but we did not care as it was so much fun and interesting. The names of the Pacifics stirred the imagination, St Leger winners, all the main characters from Sir Walter Scott's novels eg *Duke of Rothesay, Boswell, Auld Reekie* and *St Johnstoun*.

When the diesels and electrics began to appear it was a forewarning of how the railways would change and our beloved steam would eventually disappear from our national railway system. Fortunately we are indebted to the many people involved in the many preservation societies who keep steam alive from a time gone by. They all deserve a medal.

My trainspotting days started in 1948 and finished in 1955 at the age of 14 when the next chapter of my life began. But even today, I go and see the steam specials whenever possible, evoking the memories of a wonderful time of my life.

Jubilee class 4-6-0 45562 *Alberta* on an express at Holloway. This locomotive was a regular engine through Cudworth.

THE JOURNEYS FROM BARNSLEY IN THE 1950s

The 1950s was the time when services were still in full swing, prior to the rationalisation and dieselisation of services which took place towards the end of the decade.

• Barnsley to Sheffield

Barnsley Court House – Wombwell West – Elsecar for Hoyland – Wentworth for Hoyland Common (closed 2 November 1959) – Chapeltown South – Ecclesfield West (closed 6 November 1967) – Brightside (now closed) – Attercliffe Road (now closed) – Sheffield Midland.

The service was worked in the main by Stanier and Ivatt tank engines predominantly from Royston shed and on occasions working on a pull

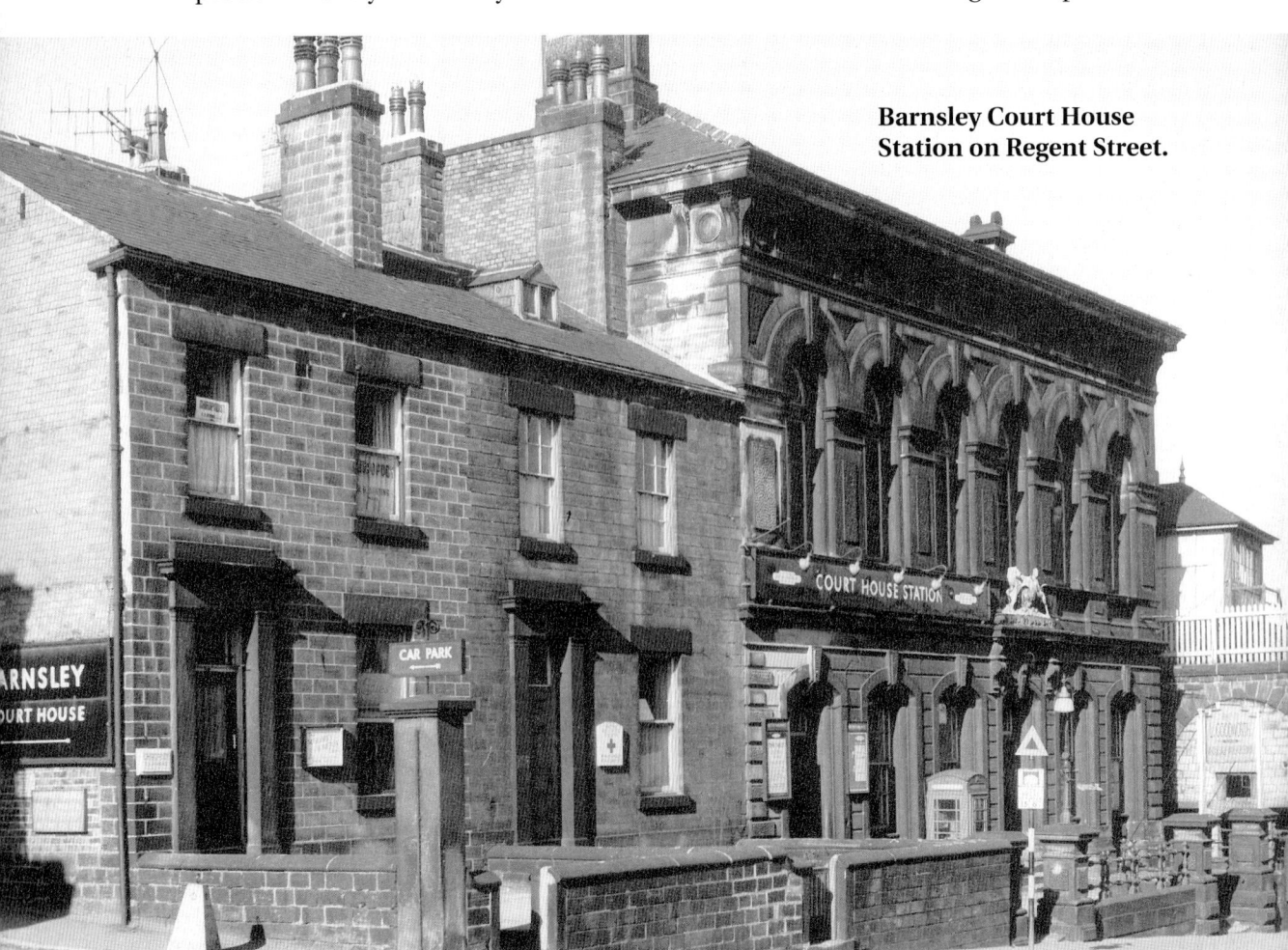

Barnsley Court House Station on Regent Street.

-and-push system. Upon closure of Wombwell Central, Wombwell West was renamed Wombwell. Chapeltown South station has been resited and rebuilt nearer to the centre adjacent to the Asda Supermarket and renamed Chapeltown. A new station has been built at Meadowhall to provide a service in the main for the Meadowhall Shopping centre.

• Penistone – Barnsley Court House – Doncaster

Penistone – Silkstone – Dodworth – Summer Lane – Barnsley Court House – Stairfoot for Ardsley – Wombwell Central – Wath Central – Mexborough – Conisborough – Doncaster.

The service was worked predominantly by J11, C13, C14, D11, and B1 classes of engines from Barnsley, Mexborough, Doncaster and Sheffield Darnall sheds. In the event of the service starting from Cleethorpes and terminating at Penistone along the same route and calling at the same stations from Doncaster, a B1 engine would be used from Immingham shed.

A Barnsley–Penistone local pauses at Silkstone station in the 1950s.

Stanier Jubilee class locomotive 45562 *Alberta* leaves the Exchange station with the Bradford–Poole Saturdays only train in 1966. The former shed lines can still be seen six years after the shed closed. A.L. Brown

• Barnsley – Leeds,

Barnsley Exchange – Darton – Haigh (closed 13 September 1965) – Crigglestone West (closed 13 September 1965) – Wakefield Kirkgate –Normanton – Altofts and Whitwood (closed early 1960s) – Woodlesford – Leeds City.

Stanier and Ivatt tank engines being the predominant motive power.

Class 37127 diesel leaves Barnsley passing over Jumble Lane crossing in the summer of 1975.

The journeys from Barnsley in the 1950s 161

Darton station as it looked in the early 20th century.

Ivatt 2-6-2T engine 41253 passes through Darton station in 1955.

Fowler 2-6-4T 42324 pauses in Wakefield Kirkgate station with a passenger train during May 1956.

Royston shed's Stanier 2-6-2T 40181 preparing to leave Leeds City station in the 1950s.

The journeys from Barnsley in the 1950s 163

A painting showing the view from the Barnsley Court House station. Ex-LNER B17 1669 *Barnsley* is shown arriving at the station. Delivered into service in 1937 as number 2869, she was renumbered 1669 in 1946. In 1949 when rebuilt to a B17/6 she was renumbered to 61669, some 21 months after becoming part of British Railways. After being condemned at Ipswich in September 1958 she was later cut up at Doncaster. Dawn Cover Productions/Artwork by G.S. Cooper.

• Barnsley Court House – Penistone

Barnsley Court House – Summer Lane – Dodworth – Silkstone – Penistone.

The motive power used was mainly C13 tank engines from Barnsley shed.

- **Barnsley Court House – Cudworth**

The only station along the line was Monk Bretton which closed in 1937. The motive power used was Stanier and Ivatt tank engines in the main, but a Midland 1P and C13 tank engines were used on occasions

- **Barnsley Court House - Sheffield Victoria**

Barnsley Court House – Stairfoot for Ardsley – Dovecliffe – Birdwell and Hoyland Common – Westwood (closed in 1940) – Chapeltown Central – Ecclesfield East – Grange Lane – Meadowhall – Tinsley (closed in 1951) – Broughton Lane (closed in 1956) – Attercliffe (closed in 1927) – Sheffield Victoria.

The service terminated on the 7 December 1953 resulting in the closure of Dovecliffe, Birdwell and Hoyland Common, Chapeltown Central , Ecclesfield East, Grange Lane and Meadowhall stations. These stations eg

Dovecliffe Station.

Birdwell and Hoyland Common station.

Birdwell and Hoyland Common, were still used for excursion traffic after official closure. The service was operated in the main by C13 tank engines from Barnsley shed

During the summer months particularly during the August Barnsley Feast week there was a significant amount of excursion traffic departing to the coastal resorts from both Barnsley stations ie Court House and Exchange along with the working mens club day trips to the coast eg Blackpool, Bridlington, Scarborough, Cleethorpes, Skegness, and Filey, which in many cases went from local stations, eg Ashfield Working Mens Club trip went from Stairfoot for Ardsley station.

The rationalisation of services during the 1950s

• The Barnsley Court House – Cudworth service terminated in June 1958.

• The Barnsley Court House – Sheffield Victoria service terminated on 7 December 1953.

• The Penistone – Barnsley – Doncaster service terminated on 29 June 1959, resulting in the closure of Silkstone, Dodworth, Summer Lane, Wombwell Central and Wath Central stations. Stairfoot for Ardsley station had closed on 16 September 1957.

• The Barnsley – Penistone service terminating at the same period as the Penistone – Barnsley – Doncaster service.

Following the requirement for extensive remedial works being required on the viaduct running adjacent to the bus station on the approach to Court House station, in early 1960 the decision was taken by British Railways to concentrate services on one station ie Barnsley Exchange by carrying out engineering works at Quarry Junction as follows , lifting the line from Stairfoot and lowering the line from Sheffield to form a new junction which allowed direct running from Sheffield to Leeds, which before had not been feasible as Sheffield trains ran into Court House station and Leeds trains ran into Exchange station. Court House station closed on 19 April 1960, it was still used for parcel and goods traffic for a period of time but was eventually demolished around 1970. A new platform was built at Exchange station as it had previously had only one, the new platform was built on part of the site of the former steam locomotive shed. The station being renamed Barnsley. Following extensive rebuilding works

The journeys from Barnsley in the 1950s 167

The sad sight of the closed Court House Station showing the line of track above the bus station. The station closed in April 1960 and was later demolished along with the viaduct. The Court House building still stands and is now a public house.

the station and the former bus station are now grouped together as the travel interchange

In 1983 the Sheffield – Huddersfield via Penistone service was rerouted through Barnsley, and new stations were built and opened at Dodworth and Silkstone Common,, near or on the site of the former stations closed back in 1959.

Before the 1950s a Barnsley – Leeds service had operated along the route of the Barnsley Coal Railway at Stairfoot, through Staincross, Royston, Ryhill and Wintersett, along with a Hull – Cudworth service using the Hull and Barnsley Railway; both services terminated in 1930 and 1932 respectively.

CONCLUSION

Well over 60 years have passed since most of the events described in these recollections occurred, and it is indeed over 50 years since the end of steam itself on Britain's railways. Lines have been lifted, stations and marshalling yards obliterated, with coal and freight traffic a shadow of what they once were. Yet the memories live on.

As you have read in the preceding pages there is still a deep warmth felt for those bygone days of harmless enjoyment, of times spent with friends as we grew up together. Trainspotting today is sneered at and unfairly ridiculed, but then it was the favourite pastime of hundreds of thousands of young boys who have never forgotten the thrill and pleasure of being at the lineside or on station platforms observing trains.

We hope this book through its words and photographs can transport you back to re-live those unforgettable days of steam, and if you are too young to remember then perhaps you will be inspired to find out more about them.

All of us wish you well in your own recollections of what those times were like. Despite the sterling efforts of preservation societies and main line steam trips, sadly we are aware that it can never be the same again.

The Exchange Station as it looked in 1967. Elvin Young